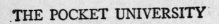

THE POCKET UNIVERSITY

ABRAHAM LINCOLN

THE
POCKET UNIVERSITY
VOLUME V   PART I

LINCOLN

EDITED BY
BLISS PERRY

PUBLISHED FOR
NELSON DOUBLEDAY, INC.
BY
DOUBLEDAY, PAGE & COMPANY
GARDEN CITY   NEW YORK
1924

Acknowledgment is due The Century Co. for permission to use selections from the text of their complete edition of the Works of Abraham Lincoln, edited by John G. Nicolay and John Hay

Preface

THE accidents of book-making have seldom resulted in a queerer companionship, within the narrow space of a single volume, than is here found in the collocation of Charles Lamb and Abraham Lincoln. Both were humorists, and each man's name begins with "L." Otherwise they were as unlike as two men well could be. But each man had it in him to write masterpieces, and each man did it. Each is loved for his purely personal qualities, qualities that would be patent had neither man written a single line. This personal affection enters, no doubt, into the literary judgment of our generation. Lamb's editors and biographers, —of whom Canon Ainger and E. V. Lucas deserve the deepest gratitude of the public,—write of him like lovers and disciples. Lincoln's biographers are now legion, and the roll-call of their names cannot be attempted here. It is enough to say that the tendency to make of Lincoln our national saint and hero—and no nation should desire a finer one!—needs, after all, the constant correction of those investigators who are gathering every scrap of actual evidence in order to record a faithful picture of a man. We can never have too many

Preface

close and fearless portrayals of the real Lincoln. Yet Lincoln is not to be understood without long and devoted reading of his utterances. The pages in the present volume are enough to serve as a key to his nature. The richness of the treasure which the key opens no one is now likely to deny.

1924.   B. P.

" He knew to bide his time.
And can his fame abide,
Still patient in his simple faith sublime,
Till the wise years decide.
Great captains, with their guns and drums,
Disturb our judgment for the hour,
But at last silence comes ;
These all are gone, and, standing like a
tower,
Our children shall behold his fame,
The kindly-earnest, brave, foreseeing man,
Sagacious, patient, dreading praise, not
blame,
New birth of our new soil, the first Ameri-
can."

LOWELL, *Commemoration Ode.*

Contents

Contents

Editor's Introduction

' It is not too much to say of him [Lincoln] that he is among the greatest masters of prose ever produced by the English race."—*The (London) Spectator*.

IT is said that Nathaniel Hawthorne was once asked the secret of his style. That consummate writer replied—no doubt with one of his inscrutable smiles—" It is the result of a great deal of practice. It comes from the desire to tell the simple truth as honestly and vividly as I can." The flawless perfection of Lincoln's style in his noblest utterances eludes a final analysis as completely as the exquisite pages of our great romancer, yet in striving to understand some of the causes of that perfection we may use the hint which Hawthorne has given us.

Lincoln had " a great deal of practice" in the art of speech long before his debates against Douglas made him known to the nation : endless talks in country stores, endless jests in frontier taverns, twenty years of pleading in the circuit courts, twenty-five years of constant political discussion. His law partner has noted his incessant interest in the precise meaning of words. His reputation for clear statement to

Introduction

a jury was the result of his passion for putting
ideas into language "plain enough for any boy
to comprehend." Lincoln's mind worked slowly, and he was long in finding the words that
exactly expressed his thoughts, but when he
had once hit upon the word or phrase he never
forgot it. "He read less and thought more
than any man in the country," says Herndon
with a sort of pride, and it should be remembered that throughout his gradual development
as a master of his mother tongue he was pre-
occupied, not with words for their own sake,
but solely with words as the garb of ideas.

Furthermore, Lincoln's mental characteristics
illustrate with singular force the remark of
Hawthorne that style is the result of a desire to
tell the simple truth as honestly and vividly as
one can. He was "Honest Abe;" not indeed
so innocent and frank and unsophisticated as
many people believed; not a man who told all
he knew, by any means; but yet a man essentially fair-minded. He looked into the nature
of things. He read human nature dispassion-
ately. A man of intense feeling, he was nevertheless, in mature life at least, without senti-
mentality. He was not fooled by phrases. As
a debater, he made no attempt to mislead his
audience; as President, when he found frank
conversation impossible, he told a humorous
story of more or less remote bearing upon the
subject in hand. He kept inviolate his mental
integrity. And without integrity of mind the

Introduction

would-be master of speech becomes a mere jug-
gler with words. In the letter to Thurlow
Weed concerning the Second Inaugural Address, Lincoln described that memorable utter-
ance as "a truth which I thought needed to be
told." No description could be more noble.

That Lincoln's gift of humor added much to
the vividness and homely naturalness of his
style will not be questioned. But the connection between fair-mindedness and humor is not
always remembered. The man of true humor
—not, of course, the mere joker or wit—sees all
sides of a proposition. He recognizes instinc-
tively its defects of proportion, its incongruities.
It is the great humorists who have drawn the
truest pictures of human life, because their
humor was a constant corrective against one-
sidedness. Lincoln's mind had the impartial-
ity, the freedom from prejudice, the flexibility
of sympathy, which belongs to the humorist
alone.

It has sometimes been argued that his fondness for story-telling showed a deficient com-
mand of language ; that knowing his inability
to express his ideas directly, he conveyed them
indirectly by an anecdote. It would probably
be nearer the truth to say that the stories were
a proof of his understanding of the limitations
of language. He divined the boundaries of expression through formal speech, and knew
when a picture, a parable, would best serve his
turn.

Introduction

As great responsibilities came to rest upon him, as the harassing problems of our national life pressed closer and closer, the lonely President grew more clear-eyed and certain of his course. The politician was lost in the statesman. His whole life, indeed, was a process of enfranchisement from selfish and narrow views. He stood at last on a serener height than other men of his epoch, breathing an ampler air, perceiving more truly the eternal realities. And his style changed as the man changed. What he saw and felt at his solitary final post he has in part made known, through a slowly perfected instrument of expression. So transparent is the language of the Gettysburg Address that one may read through it, as through a window, Lincoln's wise and gentle and unselfish heart. Other praise is needless.

The selections included in this volume are designed to illustrate the steady development of Lincoln's literary power. They begin with a few specimens of his earlier style, which was direct, forceful, and manly, but not markedly better than that of many of his contemporaries.

With the Springfield speech of June 16, 1858, Lincoln entered upon a new phase of his career. Its careful enunciation of a great political principle made it the turning-point of a memorable campaign. The significance of its opening paragraph, in particular, has been discussed in the prefatory note to the speech itself, and need not be repeated here. The space-limit of the

Introduction

volumes in this series forbids the presentation of any of the entire speeches of the joint debates with Douglas, and so closely inter-related, so full of allusion and cross reference are all of those speeches that detached paragraphs would give little conception of the qualities displayed by either of the debaters. The Cooper Union speech of February 25, 1860, however, goes over much of the ground of the Douglas debates.

The remaining speeches in the volume belong to Lincoln's career as President. They range from the most informal addresses to the Inaugural. The Emancipation Proclamation is also included. The letters exhibit still another side of Lincoln's strange and fascinating individuality. In compression and clear-cut force, in their humor and homely pathos, in their shrewd knowledge of character, these letters are among the most extraordinary ever written. While they afford new glimpses into Lincoln's nature, it is true of them, as it is of his other writings, that they express without explaining the secret of his personality. One closes a volume of Lincoln's addresses and letters with something of the feeling that Walt Whitman has uttered with regard to Lincoln's portraits: "None of the artists or pictures has caught the deep though subtle and indirect expression of this man's face. *There is something else there.*"

BLISS PERRY.

volumes in this series forbids the presentation
of any of the entire speeches of the joint debates
with Douglas and so closely inter-related, so
... allusion and cross-references are all of
... those speeches that detached paragraphs would
give little conception of the qualities displayed
by ... of the debate. The Cooper Union
speech of February 25, 1860, however, goes
over much of the ground of the Douglas debates.

The remaining ... are the volume belong
to Lincoln's career as President. They range
from the most informal addresses to the Inaugural. The Emancipation Proclamation is
also included, ... which exhibit still another
side of Lincoln's ... and fascinating individuality. In composition and clear and force,
in their humor and homely pathos, in their
... ... of rhetoric, these letters
are among the most extraordinary ever written.
... ... new ... ... Lincoln's
nature, ... of feelings ... of his other
... ... that they express without explaining
the secret of his personality. One ... a volume of Lincoln's addresses and letters with
something of the feeling that Walt Whitman
expressed with regard to Lincoln's portraits
... None of the artists or pictures has caught
... ... subtle and ... expression
of this man's face. There ... something else
there."

Bliss Perry

xiii

Selected Speeches

Selections from Lincoln's Speeches and Letters

The Whigs and the Mexican War

July 27, 1848

[An extract from a speech delivered in the House of Representatives while Lincoln was a Congressman from Illinois. The speech was in support of General Taylor, the Whig candidate for the Presidency. Lincoln had opposed President Polk's declaration of war against Mexico, had introduced resolutions of inquiry on that subject, and made a strong speech on January 12, 1848, explaining his own attitude. The speech of July 27 was full of wit, at times more caustic than refined. The extract here presented sums up clearly Lincoln's views as to the Mexican War, and is a good example of his best parliamentary style at this stage of his career.]

BUT, as General Taylor is, *par excellence*, the hero of the Mexican War, and as you Democrats say we Whigs have always opposed the war, you think it must be very awkward and embarrassing for us to go for General Taylor. The declaration that we have always opposed the war is true or false, according as one may understand the term "oppose the war." If to say "the war was unnecessarily and unconstitutionally commenced by the President" be opposing the war, then the Whigs have very generally opposed it. Whenever they have spoken at all, they have said this; and they have said it on what has appeared good reason to them. The marching an army into the midst of a peaceful Mexican settlement, frightening the inhabitants away, leaving their growing crops and other property to destruction, to you may appear a perfectly amiable, peaceful, unprovoking procedure; but it does not appear so to us. So to call such an act, to us appears no other than a naked, impudent absurdity, and we speak of it accordingly. But if, when the war had begun, and had become the cause of the country, the giving of our money and our blood, in common with yours, was support of the war, then it is not true that we have always opposed the war. With few individual exceptions, you have constantly had our votes here for all the necessary supplies. And, more than this, you have had the services, the blood, and the lives of our political brethren in every trial and on every field. The beardless boy and the mature man, the humble and the distinguished—you have had them. Through suffering and death, by disease and in battle, they have endured and fought and fell with you. Clay and Webster each gave a son, never to be returned. From the State of my own residence, besides other worthy but less known Whig names, we sent Marshall, Morrison, Baker, and Hardin; they

4

all fought, and one fell, and in the fall of that
one we lost our best Whig man. Nor were the
Whigs few in number, or laggard in the day of
danger. In that fearful, bloody, breathless
struggle at Buena Vista, where each man's hard
task was to beat back five foes or die himself,
of the five high officers who perished, four were
Whigs.

In speaking of this, I mean no odious com-
parison between the lion-hearted Whigs and
the Democrats who fought there. On other
occasions, and among the lower officers and
privates on that occasion, I doubt not the proportion was different. I wish to do justice to
all. I think of all those brave men as Americans, in whose proud fame, as an American, I
too have a share. Many of them, Whigs and
Democrats, are my constituents and personal
friends ; and I thank them,—more than thank
them,—one and all, for the high imperishable
honor they have conferred on our common
State.

But the distinction between the cause of the
President in beginning the war, and the cause
of the country after it was begun, is a distinction which you cannot perceive. To you the
President and the country seem to be all one.
You are interested to see no distinction between
them ; and I venture to suggest that probably
your interest blinds you a little. We see the
distinction, as we think, clearly enough ; and
our friends who have fought in the war have

no difficulty in seeing it also. What those who
have fallen would say, were they alive and
here, of course we can never know; but with
those who have returned there is no difficulty.
Colonel Haskell and Major Gaines, members
here, both fought in the war, and one of them
underwent extraordinary perils and hardships;
still they, like all other Whigs here, vote, on
the record, that the war was unnecessarily and
unconstitutionally commenced by the President. And even General Taylor himself, the
noblest Roman of them all, has declared that
as a citizen, and particularly as a soldier, it is
sufficient for him to know that his country is at
war with a foreign nation, to do all in his power
to bring it to a speedy and honorable termination by the most vigorous and energetic operations, without inquiry about its justice, or anything else connected with it.

Mr. Speaker, let our Democratic friends be
comforted with the assurance that we are content with our position, content with our company, and content with our candidate; and
that although they, in their generous sympathy,
think we ought to be miserable, we really are
not, and that they may dismiss the great anxiety they have on our account.

Notes for a Law Lecture

July 1, 1850

[These notes show Lincoln's power of straight-forward statement and his good sense. They are of additional interest as indicating his attitude toward professional success.]

I AM not an accomplished lawyer. I find quite as much material for a lecture in those points wherein I have failed as in those wherein I have been moderately successful. The leading rule for the lawyer, as for the man of every other calling, is diligence. Leave nothing for to-morrow which can be done to-day. Never let your correspondence fall behind. Whatever piece of business you have in hand, before stopping, do all the labor pertaining to it which can then be done. When you bring a common-law suit, if you have the facts for doing so, write the declaration at once. If a law point be involved, examine the books, and note the authority you rely on upon the declaration itself, where you are sure to find it when wanted. The same of defenses and pleas. In business not likely to be litigated,—ordinary collection cases, foreclosures, partitions, and the like,—

make all examinations of titles, and note them, and even draft orders and decrees in advance. This course has a triple advantage ; it avoids omissions and neglect, saves your labor when once done, performs the labor out of court when you have leisure, rather than in court when you have not. Extemporaneous speaking should be practised and cultivated. It is the lawyer's avenue to the public. However able and faithful he may be in other respects, people are slow to bring him business if he cannot make a speech. And yet there is not a more fatal error to young lawyers than relying too much on speech-making. If any one, upon his rare powers of speaking, shall claim an exemption from the drudgery of the law, his case is a failure in advance.

Discourage litigation. Persuade your neighbors to compromise whenever you can. Point out to them how the nominal winner is often a real loser—in fees, expenses, and waste of time. As a peacemaker the lawyer has a superior opportunity of being a good man. There will still be business enough.

Never stir up litigation. A worse man can scarcely be found than one who does this. Who can be more nearly a fiend than he who habitually overhauls the register of deeds in search of defects in titles, whereon to stir up strife, and put money in his pocket? A moral tone ought to be infused into the profession which should drive such men out of it.

8

Notes for a Law Lecture

The matter of fees is important, far beyond the mere question of bread and butter involved. Properly attended to, fuller justice is done to both lawyer and client. An exorbitant fee should never be claimed. As a general rule never take your whole fee in advance, nor any more than a small retainer. When fully paid beforehand, you are more than a common mortal if you can feel the same interest in the case, as if something was still in prospect for you, as well as for your client. And when you lack interest in the case the job will very likely lack skill and diligence in the performance. Settle the amount of fee and take a note in advance. Then you will feel that you are working for something, and you are sure to do your work faithfully and well. Never sell a fee note—at least not before the consideration service is performed. It leads to negligence and dishonesty—negligence by losing interest in the case, and dishonesty in refusing to refund when you have allowed the consideration to fail.

There is a vague popular belief that lawyers are necessarily dishonest. I say vague, because when we consider to what extent confidence and honors are reposed in and conferred upon lawyers by the people, it appears improbable that their impression of dishonesty is very distinct and vivid. Yet the impression is common, almost universal. Let no young man choosing the law for a calling for a moment yield to the popular belief—resolve to be honest at all

events ; and if in your own judgment you cannot be an honest lawyer, resolve to be honest
without being a lawyer. Choose some other
occupation, rather than one in the choosing of
which you do, in advance, consent to be **a**
knave.

Abraham Lincoln

Fragment on Slavery

July 1, 1854

[From early manhood Lincoln's sympathies had been strongly enlisted on behalf of the slaves. The contrast between slave labor and free labor has never been stated more tersely and vividly than here. The sentence, "Twenty-five years ago I was a hired laborer," should be noted.]

EQUALITY in society alike beats inequality, whether the latter be of the British aristocratic sort or of the domestic slavery sort. We know Southern men declare that their slaves are better off than hired laborers amongst us. How little they know whereof they speak! There is no permanent class of hired laborers amongst us. Twenty-five years ago I was a hired laborer. The hired laborer of yesterday labors on his own account to-day, and will hire others to labor for him to-morrow. Advancement—improvement in condition—is the order of things in a society of equals. As labor is the common burden of our race, so the effort of some to shift their share of the burden onto the shoulders of others is the great durable curse of the race.

11

Originally a curse for transgression upon the whole race, when, as by slavery, it is concentrated on a part only, it becomes the double-refined curse of God upon his creatures.

Free labor has the inspiration of hope ; pure slavery has no hope. The power of hope upon human exertion and happiness is wonderful. The slave-master himself has a conception of it, and hence the system of tasks among slaves. The slave whom you cannot drive with the lash to break seventy-five pounds of hemp in a day, if you will task him to break a hundred, and promise him pay for all he does over, he will break you a hundred and fifty. You have substituted hope for the rod. And yet perhaps it does not occur to you that to the extent of your gain in the case, you have given up the slave system and adopted the free system of labor.

The Dred Scott Decision and the Declaration of Independence

June 26, 1857

[This is an extract from a speech delivered in Springfield, Ill. It was intended as a reply to a speech of Stephen A. Douglas two weeks earlier upon the subject of slavery in the Territories. Douglas was the author of the Kansas-Nebraska bill, passed in 1854, which gave the Territories the right to decide whether they would have slavery. The Dred Scott decision was published by the Supreme Court of the United States in 1857, and was to the effect that a slave or the descendant of a slave could not be a citizen of the United States or have any standing in the Federal courts. Lincoln contrasts the spirit of this decision with that of the Declaration of Independence, with a skill and force that will be apparent to every reader. He repeated the substance of the argument over and over again in his joint debates with Douglas in the following year.]

I HAVE said, in substance, that the Dred Scott decision was in part based on assumed historical facts which were not really true, and I ought not to leave the subject without giving some reasons for saying this ; I therefore give an instance or two, which I think fully sustain me. Chief Justice Taney, in delivering the opinion of the majority of the court, insists at great length that negroes were no part of the people who made, or for whom was made, the Declaration of Independence, or the Constitution of the United States.

On the contrary, Judge Curtis, in his dissenting opinion, shows that in five of the then thirteen States—to wit, New Hampshire, Massachusetts, New York, New Jersey, and North Carolina—free negroes were voters, and in proportion to their numbers had the same part in making the Constitution that the white people had. He shows this with so much particularity as to leave no doubt of its truth ; and as a sort of conlusion on that point, holds the following language :

" The Constitution was ordained and established by the people of the United States, through the action, in each State, of those persons who were qualified by its laws to act thereon in behalf of themselves and all other citizens of the State. In some of the States, as we have seen, colored persons were among those qualified by law to act on the subject. These colored persons were not only included in the body of ' the people of the United States ' by whom the Constitution was ordained and established ; but in at least five of the States they had the power to act, and doubtless did act, by their suffrages, upon the question of its adoption."

Again, Chief Justice Taney says :

" It is difficult at this day to realize the state of public opinion, in relation to that unfortunate race, which prevailed in the civilized and en-

lightened portions of the world at the time of
the Declaration of Independence, and when the
Constitution of the United States was framed
and adopted."

And again, after quoting from the Declaration, he says :

" The general words above quoted would
seem to include the whole human family, and
if they were used in a similar instrument at this
day, would be so understood."

In these the Chief Justice does not directly
assert but plainly assumes as a fact, that the
public estimate of the black man is more favorable now than it was in the days of the Revolution. This assumption is a mistake. In some
trifling particulars the condition of that race
has been ameliorated ; but as a whole, in this
country, the change between then and now is
decidedly the other way ; and their ultimate
destiny has never appeared so hopeless as in
the last three or four years. In two of the five
States—New Jersey and North Carolina—that
then gave the free negro the right of voting,
the right has since been taken away, and in a
third—New York—it has been greatly abridged ;
while it has not been extended, so far as I know,
to a single additional State, though the number
of the States has more than doubled. In those
days, as I understand, masters could, at their
own pleasure, emancipate their slaves ; but
since then such legal restraints have been made
upon emancipation as to amount almost to pro-

hibition. In those days legislatures held the unquestioned power to abolish slavery in their respective States, but now it is becoming quite fashionable for State constitutions to withhold that power from the legislatures. In those days, by common consent, the spread of the black man's bondage to the new countries was prohibited, but now Congress decides that it will not continue the prohibition, and the Supreme Court decides that it could not if it would. In those days our Declaration of Independence was held sacred by all, and thought to include all; but now, to aid in making the bondage of the negro universal and eternal, it is assailed and sneered at and construed, and hawked at and torn, till, if its framers could rise from their graves, they could not at all recognize it. All the powers of earth seem rapidly combining against him. Mammon is after him, ambition follows, philosophy follows, and the theology of the day is fast joining the cry. They have him in his prison-house; they have searched his person, and left no prying instrument with him One after another they have closed the heavy iron doors upon him; and now they have him, as it were, bolted in with a lock of a hundred keys, which can never be unlocked without the concurrence of every key—the keys in the hands of a hundred different men, and they scattered to a hundred different and distant places; and they stand musing as to what invention, in all the dominions of mind and man ter, can be produced to make the impossibility of his escape more complete than it is.

It is grossly incorrect to say or assume that the public estimate of the negro is more favorable now than it was at the origin of the government.

Three years and a half ago, Judge Douglas brought forward his famous Nebraska bill. The country was at once in a blaze. He scorned all opposition, and carried it through Congress. Since then he has seen himself superseded in a presidential nomination by one indorsing the general doctrine of his measure, but at the same time standing clear of the odium of its untimely agitation and its gross breach of national faith ; and he has seen that successful rival constitutionally elected, not by the strength of friends, but by the division of adversaries, being in a popular minority of nearly four hundred thousand votes. He has seen his chief aids in his own State, Shields and Richardson, politically speaking, successively tried, convicted, and executed for an offense not their own, but his. And now he sees his own case standing next on the docket for trial.

There is a natural disgust in the minds of nearly all white people at the idea of an indiscriminate amalgamation of the white and black races ; and Judge Douglas evidently is basing his chief hope upon the chances of his being able to appropriate the benefit of this disgust to himself. If he can, by much drumming and repeating, fasten the odium of that idea upon his adversaries, he thinks he can struggle through the storm. He therefore clings to this hope, as a drowning man to the last plank. He makes an occasion for lugging it in from the opposition to the Dred Scott decision. He finds the Republicans insisting that the Declaration of Independence includes *all* men, black as well as white, and forthwith he boldly denies that it includes negroes at all, and proceeds to argue gravely that all who contend it does, do so only because they want to vote, and eat, and sleep, and marry with negroes! He will have it that they cannot be consistent else. Now I protest against the counterfeit logic which concludes that, because I do not want a black woman for a slave I must necessarily want her for a wife. I need not have her for either. I can just leave her alone. In some respects she certainly is not my equal; but in her natural right to eat the bread she earns with her own hands without asking leave of any one else, she is my equal, and the equal of all others.

Chief Justice Taney, in his opinion in the Dred Scott case, admits that the language of the Declaration is broad enough to include the whole human family, but he and Judge Douglas argue that the authors of that instrument did not intend to include negroes, by the fact that they did not at once actually place them on an equality with the whites. Now this grave argument comes to just nothing at all, by the other

Dred Scott Decision

fact that they did not at once, or ever after-ward, actually place all white people on an equality with one another. And this is the staple argument of both the chief justice and the senator for doing this obvious violence to the plain, unmistakable language of the Declaration.

I think the authors of that notable instrument intended to include *all* men, but they did not intend to declare all men equal *in all respects*. They did not mean to say all were equal in color, size, intellect, moral developments, or social capacity. They defined with tolerable distinctness in what respects they did consider all men created equal—equal with " certain inalienable rights, among which are life, liberty, and the pursuit of happiness." This they said, and this they meant. They did not mean to assert the obvious untruth that all were then actually enjoying that equality, nor yet that they were about to confer it immediately upon them. In fact, they had no power to confer such a boon. They meant simply to declare the right, so that enforcement of it might follow as fast as circumstances should permit.

They meant to set up a standard maxim for free society, which should be familiar to all, and revered by all ; constantly looked to, constantly labored for, and even though never perfectly attained, constantly approximated, and thereby constantly spreading and deepening its influence and augmenting the happiness and

value of life to all people of all colors everywhere. The assertion that "all men are cre
ated equal" was of no practical use in effecting
our separation from Great Britain; and it was
placed in the Declaration not for that, but for
future use. Its authors meant it to be—as,
thank God, it is now proving itself—a stum-
bling-block to all those who in after-times might
seek to turn a free people back into the hateful
paths of despotism. They knew the proneness
of prosperity to breed tyrants, and they meant
when such should reappear in this fair land and
commence their vocation, they should find left
for them at least one hard nut to crack.

I have now briefly expressed my view of the
meaning and object of that part of the Declaration of Independence which declares that "all
men are created equal."

Now let us hear Judge Douglas's view of the
same subject, as I find it in the printed report
of his late speech. Here it is:

"No man can vindicate the character, motives, and conduct of the signers of the Declaration of Independence, except upon the hypothesis that they referred to the white race alone,
and not to the African, when they declared all
men to have been created equal, that they
were speaking of British subjects on this continent being equal to British subjects born and
residing in Great Britain; that they were entitled to the same inalienable rights, and among
them were enumerated life, liberty, and the
pursuit of happiness. The Declaration was
adopted for the purpose of justifying the colo-

nists in the eyes of the civilized world in with
drawing their allegiance from the British crown,
and dissolving their connection with the mother
country."

My good friends, read that carefully over
some leisure hour, and ponder well upon it ;
see what a mere wreck—mangled ruin—it
makes of our once glorious Declaration.

"They were speaking of British subjects on
this continent being equal to British subjects
born and residing in Great Britain !" Why,
according to this, not only negroes but white
people outside of Great Britain and America
were not spoken of in that instrument. The
English, Irish, and Scotch, along with white
Americans, were included, to be sure, but the
French, Germans, and other white people of
the world are all gone to pot along with the
judge's inferior races !

I had thought the Declaration pro
thing better than the condition
jects ; but no, it only meant thon,
equal to them in their own oppressed and unequal condition. According to that, it gave no
promise that, having kicked off the king and
lords of Great Britain, we should not at once
be saddled with a king and lords of our own.

I had thought the Declaration contemplated
the progressive improvement in the condition
of all men everywhere ; but no, it merely " was
adopted for the purpose of justifying the colo-
nists in the eyes of the civilized world in with

drawing their allegiance from the British crown, and dissolving their connection with the mother country." Why, that object having been effected some eighty years ago, the Declaration is of no practical use now—mere rubbish—old wadding left to rot on the battle-field after the victory is won.

I understand you are preparing to celebrate the "Fourth," to-morrow week. What for? The doings of that day had no reference to the present; and quite half of you are not even descendants of those who were referred to at that day. But I suppose you will celebrate, and will even go so far as to read the Declaration. Suppose, after you read it once in the old-fashioned way, you read it once more with Judge Douglas's version. It will then run thus: "We hold these truths to be self-evident, that all British subjects who were on this continent eighty-one years ago, were created equal to all British subjects born and then residing in Great Britain."

And now I appeal to all—to Democrats as well as others—are you really willing that the Declaration shall thus be frittered away?—thus left no more, at most, than an interesting memorial of the dead past?—thus shorn of its vitality and practical value, and left without the germ or even the suggestion of the individual rights of man in it?

Springfield Speech

June 16, 1858

Speech delivered at Springfield, Illinois, at the close of the Republican State Convention by which Mr. Lincoln had been named as their candidate for United States Senator.

[The opening paragraph of this speech was prepared with the most extreme care, and probably did more to influence Lincoln's political future than anything he ever wrote. His best friends thought it impolitic to utter the sentiment that the "government cannot endure permanently half slave and half free."

For the immediate purpose of that campaign they were right, for this paragraph, in the opinion of many good judges, was the cause of Lincoln's defeat by Douglas. But the constant discussion of those sentences in the great series of joint debates with Douglas during the summer and autumn brought Lincoln's views before the whole country, and was an important element in his selection as the Republican candidate for the Presidency in 1860. The entire speech, read in the light of subsequent history, affords remarkable evidence not only of Lincoln's shrewdness as a party leader, but of his political wisdom in the highest sense.]

Mr. President and Gentlemen of the Convention: If we could first know where we are, and whither we are tending, we could better judge what to do, and how to do it. We are now far into the fifth year since a policy was initiated with the avowed object and confident promise of putting an end to slavery agitation. Under the operation of that policy, that agitation has not only not ceased, but has constantly augmented. In my opinion, it will not cease until a crisis shall have been reached and passed. "A house divided against itself cannot stand." I believe this government cannot endure permanently half slave and half free. I do not expect the Union to be dissolved—I do not expect the house to fall—but I do expect it will cease to be divided. It will become all one thing, or all the other. Either the opponents of slavery will arrest the further spread of it, and place it where the public mind shall rest in the belief that it is in the course of ultimate extinction ; or its advocates will push it forward till it shall become alike lawful in all the States, old as well as new, North as well as South.

Have we no tendency to the latter condition ?

Let any one who doubts carefully contemplate that now almost complete legal combination—piece of machinery, so to speak—compounded of the Nebraska doctrine and the Dred Scott decision. Let him consider not only what work the machinery is adapted to do, and how well adapted ; but also let him study the history of its construction, and trace, if he can, or rather fail, if he can, to trace the evidences of design and concert of action among its chief architects, from the beginning.

The new year of 1854 found slavery excluded from more than half the States by State constitutions, and from most of the national territory by congressional prohibition. Four days later commenced the struggle which ended in repealing that congressional prohibition. This opened all the national territory to slavery, and was the first point gained.

But, so far, Congress only had acted ; and an indorsement by the people, real or apparent, was indispensable to save the point already gained and give chance for more.

This necessity had not been overlooked, but had been provided for, as well as might be, in the notable argument of "squatter sovereignty," otherwise called "sacred right of self government," which latter phrase, though expressive of the only rightful basis of any government. was so perverted in this attempted use of it as to amount to just this : That if any one man choose to enslave another. no third man shall be allowed to object. That argument was incorporated into the Nebraska bill itself, in the language which follows : " It being the true intent and meaning of this act not to legislate slavery into any Territory or State, nor to exclude it therefrom ; but to leave the people thereof perfectly free to form and regulate their domestic institutions in their own way, subject only to the Constitution of the United States."

Then opened the roar of loose declamation in favor of "squatter sovereignty" and "sacred right of self-government." "But," said opposition members, "let us amend the bill so as to expressly declare that the people of the Territory may exclude slavery." "Not we," said the friends of the measure; and down they voted the amendment.

While the Nebraska bill was passing through Congress, a law case involving the question of a negro's freedom, by reason of his owner having voluntarily taken him first into a free State and then into a Territory covered by the congressional prohibition, and held him as a slave for a long time in each, was passing through the United States Circuit Court for the District of Missouri; and both Nebraska bill and lawsuit were brought to a decision in the same month of May, 1854. The negro's name was Dred Scott, which name now designates the decision finally made in the case. Before the then next presidential election, the law case came to and was argued in the Supreme Court of the United States; but the decision of it was deferred until after the election. Still, before the election, Senator Trumbull, on the floor of the Senate, requested the leading advocate of the Nebraska bill to state his opinion whether the people of a Territory can constitutionally exclude slavery from their limits; and the latter answered: "That is a question for the Supreme Court."

The election came. Mr. Buchanan was elected, and the indorsement, such as it was, secured. That was the second point gained.
The indorsement, however, fell short of a clear
popular majority by nearly four hundred thousand votes, and so, perhaps, was not over-
whelmingly reliable and satisfactory. The outgoing President, in his last annual message, as
impressively as possible echoed back upon the
people the weight and authority of the indorsement. The Supreme Court met again ; did not
announce their decision, but ordered a reargument. The presidential inauguration came,
and still no decision of the court ; but the incoming President in his inaugural address fer-
vently exhorted the people to abide by the forth-
coming decision, whatever it might be. Then,
in a few days, came the decision.

The reputed author of the Nebraska bill finds
an early occasion to make a speech at this capital indorsing the Dred Scott decision, and
vehemently denouncing all opposition to it.
The new President, too, seizes the early occasion of the Silliman letter to indorse and strongly
construe that decision, and to express his astonishment that any different view had ever been
entertained !

At length a squabble springs up between the
President and the author of the Nebraska bill,
on the mere question of fact, whether the
Lecompton constitution was or was not, in any
just sense, made by the people of Kansas ; and

Abraham Lincoln

in that quarrel the latter declares that all he
wants is a fair vote for the people, and that he
cares not whether slavery be voted down or
voted up. I do not understand his declaration
that he cares not whether slavery be voted
down or voted up to be intended by him other
than as an apt definition of the policy he would
impress upon the public mind—the principle
for which he declares he has suffered so much,
and is ready to suffer to the end. And well
may he cling to that principle. If he has any
parental feeling, well may he cling to it. That
principle is the only shred left of his original
Nebraska doctrine. Under the Dred Scott decision "squatter sovereignty" squatted out of
existence, tumbled down like temporary scaffolding,—like the mold at the foundry, served
through one blast and fell back into loose sand,
—helped to carry an election, and then was
kicked to the winds. His late joint struggle
with the Republicans against the Lecompton
constitution involves nothing of the original
Nebraska doctrine. That struggle was made
on a point—the right of a people to make their
own constitution—upon which he and the Re
publicans have never differed.

The several points of the Dred Scott decision,
in connection with Senator Douglas's " care
not" policy, constitute the piece of machinery
in its present state of advancement. This was
the third point gained. The working points of
that machinery are :

(1) That no negro slave, imported as such from Africa, and no descendant of such slave, can ever be a citizen of any State, in the sense of that term as used in the Constitution of the United States. This point is made in order to deprive the negro in every possible event of the benefit of that provision of the United States Constitution which declares that "the citizens of each State shall be entitled to all the privileges and immunities of citizens in the several States."

(2) That, "subject to the Constitution of the United States," neither Congress nor a territorial legislature can exclude slavery from any United States Territory. This point is made in order that individual men may fill up the Territories with slaves, without danger of losing them as property, and thus enhance the chances of permanency to the institution through all the future.

(3) That whether the holding a negro in actual slavery in a free State makes him free as against the holder, the United States courts will not decide, but will leave to be decided by the courts of any slave State the negro may be forced into by the master. This point is made not to be pressed immediately, but, if acquiesced in for a while and apparently indorsed by the people at an election, then to sustain the logical conclusion that what Dred Scott's master might lawfully do with Dred Scott in the free State of Illinois, every other master may law-

fully do with any other one or one thousand slaves in Illinois or in any other free State.

Auxiliary to all this, and working hand in hand with it, the Nebraska doctrine, or what is left of it, is to educate and mold public opin· jon, at least Northern public opinion, not to care whether slavery is voted down or voted up. This shows exactly where we now are, and partially, also, whither we are tending.

It will throw additional light on the latter, to go back and run the mind over the string of historical facts already stated. Several things will now appear less dark and mysterious than they did when they were transpiring. The people were to be left " perfectly free," " subject only to the Constitution." What the Constitution had to do with it outsiders could not then see. Plainly enough now, it was an exactly fitted niche for the Dred Scott decision to afterward come in, and declare the perfect freedom of the people to be just no freedom at all. Why was the amendment expressly declaring the right of the people voted down? Plainly enough now, the adoption of it would have spoiled the niche for the Dred Scott decision. Why was the court decision held up? Why even a senator's individual opinion withheld till after the presidential election? Plainly enough now, the speaking out then would have damaged the " perfectly free" argument upon which the election was to be carried. Why the outgoing President's felicitation on the indorsement? Why the delay of a reargument? Why the incoming President's advance exhortation in favor of the decision? These things look like the cautious patting and petting of a spirited horse preparatory to mounting him, when it is dreaded that he may give the rider a fall. And why the hasty after-indorsement of the decision by the President and others?

We cannot absolutely know that all these exact adaptations are the result of preconcert. But when we see a lot of framed timbers, different portions of which we know have been gotten out at different times and places and by different workmen,—Stephen, Franklin, Roger, and James, for instance,—and we see these timbers joined together, and see they exactly make the frame of a house or a mill, all the tenons and mortises exactly fitting, and all the lengths and proportions of the different pieces exactly adapted to their respective places, and not a piece too many or too few, not omitting even scaffolding—or, if a single piece be lacking, we see the place in the frame exactly fitted and prepared yet to bring such piece in—in such a case we find it impossible not to believe that Stephen and Franklin and Roger and James all understood one another from the beginning, and all worked upon a common plan or draft drawn up before the first blow was struck.

It should not be overlooked that, by the Nebraska bill, the people of a State as well as Territory were to be left " perfectly free," " sub-

ject only to the Constitution." Why mention
a State? They were legislating for Territories,
and not for or about States. Certainly the people of a State are and ought to be subject to
the Constitution of the United States; but why
is mention of this lugged into this merely territorial law? Why are the people of a Territory
and the people of a State therein lumped together, and their relation to the Constitution
therein treated as being precisely the same?
While the opinion of the court, by Chief Justice
Taney, in the Dred Scott case, and the separate
opinions of all the concurring judges, expressly
declare that the Constitution of the United
States neither permits Congress nor a territorial legislature to exclude slavery from any
United States Territory, they all omit to declare whether or not the same Constitution permits a State, or the people of a State, to exclude
it. Possibly, this is a mere omission; but who
can be quite sure, if McLean or Curtis had
sought to get into the opinion a declaration of
unlimited power in the people of a State to exclude slavery from their limits, just as Chase
and Mace sought to get such declaration, in
behalf of the people of a Territory, into the
Nebraska bill—I ask, who can be quite sure
that it would not have been voted down in the
one case as it had been in the other? The
nearest approach to the point of declaring the
power of a State over slavery is made by Judge
Nelson. He approaches it more than once,

using the precise idea, and almost the language too, of the Nebraska act. On one occasion his exact language is . " Except in cases where the power is restrained by the Constitution of the United States, the law of the State is supreme over the subject of slavery within its jurisdiction " In what cases the power of the States is so restrained by the United States Constitution is left an open question, precisely as the same question as to the restraint on the power of the Territories was left open in the Nebraska act. Put this and that together, and we have another nice little niche, which we may, ere long, see filled with another Supreme Court decision declaring that the Constitution of the United States does not permit a State to exclude slavery from its limits. And this may especially be expected if the doctrine of " care not whether slavery be voted down or voted up" shall gain upon the public mind sufficiently to give promise that such a decision can be maintained when made.

Such a decision is all that slavery now lacks of being alike lawful in all the States. Welcome, or unwelcome, such decision is probably coming, and will soon be upon us, unless the power of the present political dynasty shall be met and overthrown. We shall lie down pleasantly dreaming that the people of Missouri are on the verge of making their State free, and we shall awake to the reality instead that the Supreme Court has made Illinois a slave State.

Abraham Lincoln

To meet and overthrow the power of that dynasty is the work now before all those who would prevent that consummation. That is what we have to do. How can we best do it?

There are those who denounce us openly to their own friends, and yet whisper us softly that Senator Douglas is the aptest instrument there is with which to effect that object. They wish us to infer all from the fact that he now has a little quarrel with the present head of the dynasty; and that he has regularly voted with us on a single point upon which he and we have never differed. They remind us that he is a great man, and that the largest of us are very small ones. Let this be granted. But "a living dog is better than a dead lion." Judge Douglas, if not a dead lion for this work, is at least a caged and toothless one. How can he oppose the advances of slavery? He don't care anything about it. His avowed mission is impressing the "public heart" to care nothing about it. A leading Douglas Democratic newspaper thinks Douglas's superior talent will be needed to resist the revival of the African slave-trade. Does Douglas believe an effort to revive that trade is approaching? He has not said so. Does he really think so? But if it is, how can he resist it? For years he has labored to prove it a sacred right of white men to take negro slaves into the new Territories. Can he possibly show that it is less a sacred right to buy them where they can be bought cheapest?

And unquestionably they can be bought cheaper in Africa than in Virginia. He has done all in his power to reduce the whole question of slavery to one of a mere right of property ; and as such, how can he oppose the foreign slave-trade? How can he refuse that trade in that "property" shall be "perfectly free," unless he does it as a protection to the home production? And as the home producers will probably not ask the protection, he will be wholly without a ground of opposition.

Senator Douglas holds, we know, that a man may rightfully be wiser to-day than he was yesterday—that he may rightfully change when he finds himself wrong. But can we, for that reason, run ahead, and infer that he will make any particular change of which he, himself, has given no intimation? Can we safely base our action upon any such vague inference? Now, as ever, I wish not to misrepresent Judge Douglas's position, question his motives, or do aught that can be personally offensive to him. Whenever, if ever, he and we can come together on principle so that our great cause may have assistance from his great ability, I hope to have interposed no adventitious obstacle. But clearly, he is not now with us—he does not pretend to be—he does not promise ever to be.

Our cause, then, must be intrusted to, and conducted by, its own undoubted friends—those whose hands are free, whose hearts are in the work, who do care for the result. Two years ago the Republicans of the nation mustered over thirteen hundred thousand strong. We did this under the single impulse of resistance to a common danger, with every external circumstance against us. Of strange, discordant, and even hostile elements, we gathered from the four winds, and formed and fought the battle through, under the constant hot fire of a disciplined, proud, and pampered enemy. Did we brave all then to falter now?—now, when that same enemy is wavering, dissevered, and belligerent? The result is not doubtful. We shall not fail—if we stand firm, we shall not fail. Wise counsels may accelerate or mistakes delay it, but, sooner or later, the victory is sure to come.

Address at Cooper Institute

February 27, 1860

[This was Lincoln's first appearance before an Eastern audience. The speech cost him a great deal of labor, and was most heartily received.—See *Morse's* "*Abraham Lincoln*," I., 153–156.]

Mr. President and Fellow-citizens of New York: The facts with which I shall deal this evening are mainly old and familiar; nor is there anything new in the general use I shall make of them. If there shall be any novelty, it will be in the mode of presenting the facts, and the inferences and observations following that presentation. In his speech last autumn at Columbus, Ohio, as reported in the New York *Times*, Senator Douglas said:

" Our fathers, when they framed the government under which we live, understood this question just as well, and even better, than we do now."

I fully indorse this, and I adopt it as a text for this discourse. I so adopt it because it furnishes a precise and an agreed starting-point for a discussion between Republicans and that wing of the Democracy headed by Senator

37

Douglas. It simply leaves the inquiry : What was the understanding those fathers had of the question mentioned ?

What is the frame of government under which we live ? The answer must be, " The Constitution of the United States." That Constitution consists of the original, framed in 1787, and under which the present government first went into operation, and twelve subsequently framed amendments, the first ten of which were framed in 1789.

Who were our fathers that framed the Constitution ? I suppose the " thirty-nine" who signed the original instrument may be fairly called our fathers who framed that part of the present government. It is almost exactly true to say they framed it, and it is altogether true to say they fairly represented the opinion and sentiment of the whole nation at that time. Their names, being familiar to nearly all, and accessible to quite all, need not now be repeated.

I take these " thirty-nine," for the present, as being " our fathers who framed the government under which we live." What is the question which, according to the text, those fathers understood " just as well, and even better, than we do now" ?

It is this : Does the proper division of local from Federal authority, or anything in the Constitution, forbid our Federal Government to control as to slavery in our Federal Territories /

Address at Cooper Institute

Upon this, Senator Douglas holds the affirmative, and Republicans the negative. This affirmation and denial form an issue ; and this issue—this question—is precisely what the text declares our fathers understood " better than we." Let us now inquire whether the " thirty-nine," or any of them, ever acted upon this question ; and if they did, how they acted upon it—how they expressed that better understanding. In 1784, three years before the Constitution, the United States then owning the North-western Territory, and no other, the Congress of the Confederation had before them the question of prohibiting slavery in that Territory ; and four of the " thirty-nine" who afterward framed the Constitution were in that Congress, and voted on that question. Of these, Roger Sherman, Thomas Mifflin, and Hugh Williamson voted for the prohibition, thus showing that, in their understanding, no line dividing local from Federal authority, nor anything else, properly forbade the Federal Government to control as to slavery in Federal territory. The other of the four, James McHenry, voted against the prohibition, showing that for some cause he thought it improper to vote for it.

In 1787, still before the Constitution, but while the convention was in session framing it, and while the Northwestern Territory still was the only Territory owned by the United States, the same question of prohibiting slavery in the Territory again came before the Congress of the Confederation ; and two more of the "thirty-nine" who afterward signed the Constitution were in that Congress, and voted on the question. They were William Blount and William Few ; and they both voted for the prohibition—thus showing that in their understanding no line dividing local from Federal authority, nor anything else, properly forbade the Federal Government to control as to slavery in Federal territory. This time the prohibition became a law, being part of what is now well known as the ordinance of '87.

The question of Federal control of slavery in the Territories seems not to have been directly before the convention which framed the original Constitution ; and hence it is not recorded that the "thirty-nine," or any of them, while engaged on that instrument, expressed any opinion on that precise question.

In 1789, by the first Congress which sat under the Constitution, an act was passed to enforce the ordinance of '87, including the prohibition of slavery in the Northwestern Territory. The bill for this act was reported by one of the "thirty-nine"—Thomas Fitzsimmons, then a member of the House of Representatives from Pennsylvania. It went through all its stages without a word of opposition, and finally passed both branches without ayes and nays, which is equivalent to a unanimous passage. In this Congress there were sixteen of the thirty-nine fathers who framed the original Constitution.

They were John Langdon, Nicholas Gilman, Wm. S. Johnson, Roger Sherman, Robert Morris, Thos. Fitzsimmons, William Few, Abraham Baldwin, Rufus King, William Paterson, George Clymer, Richard Bassett, George Read, Pierce Butler, Daniel Carroll, and James Madison.

This shows that, in their understanding, no line dividing local from Federal authority, nor anything in the Constitution, properly forbade Congress to prohibit slavery in the Federal territory ; else both their fidelity to correct principle, and their oath to support the Constitution, would have constrained them to oppose the prohibition.

Again, George Washington, another of the "thirty-nine," was then President of the United States, and as such approved and signed the bill, thus completing its validity as a law, and thus showing that, in his understanding, no line dividing local from Federal authority, nor anything in the Constitution, forbade the Federal Government to control as to slavery in Federal territory.

No great while after the adoption of the original Constitution, North Carolina ceded to the Federal Government the country now constituting the State of Tennessee ; and a few years later Georgia ceded that which now constitutes the States of Mississippi and Alabama. In both deeds of cession it was made a condition by the ceding States that the Federal Government should not prohibit slavery in the ceded country. Besides this, slavery was then actually in the ceded country. Under these circumstances, Congress, on taking charge of these countries, did not absolutely prohibit slavery within them. But they did interfere with it—take control of it—even there, to a certain extent. In 1798 Congress organized the Territory of Mississippi. In the act of organization they prohibited the bringing of slaves into the Territory from any place without the United States, by fine, and giving freedom to slaves so brought. This act passed both branches of Congress without yeas and nays. In that Congress were three of the "thirty-nine" who framed the original Constitution. They were John Langdon, George Read, and Abraham Baldwin. They all probably voted for it. Certainly they would have placed their opposition to it upon record if, in their understanding, any line dividing local from Federal authority, or anything in the Constitution, properly forbade the Federal Government to control as to slavery in Federal territory.

In 1803 the Federal Government purchased the Louisiana country. Our former territorial acquisitions came from certain of our own States; but this Louisiana country was acquired from a foreign nation. In 1804 Congress gave a territorial organization to that part of it which now constitutes the State of Louisiana. New Orleans, lying within that part, was an old and comparatively large city.

Address at Cooper Institute

There were other considerable towns and settlements, and slavery was extensively and thoroughly intermingled with the people. Congress did not, in the Territorial Act, prohibit slavery; but they did interfere with it—take control of it—in a more marked and extensive way than they did in the case of Mississippi. The substance of the provision therein made in relation to slaves was :

1st. That no slave should be imported into the Territory from foreign parts.

2d. That no slave should be carried into it who had been imported into the United States since the first day of May, 1798.

3d. That no slave should be carried into it, except by the owner, and for his own use as a settler ; the penalty in all the cases being a fine upon the violator of the law, and freedom to the slave.

This act also was passed without ayes or nays. In the Congress which passed it there were two of the "thirty-nine." They were Abraham Baldwin and Jonathan Dayton. As stated in the case of Mississippi, it is probable they both voted for it. They would not have allowed it to pass without recording their opposition to it if, in their understanding, it violated either the line properly dividing local from Federal authority, or any provision of the Constitution.

In 1819-20 came and passed the Missouri question. Many votes were taken, by yeas and nays, in both branches of Congress, upon the various phases of the general question. Two of the "thirty-nine"—Rufus King and Charles Pinckney—were members of that Congress. Mr. King steadily voted for slavery prohibition and against all compromises, while Mr. Pinckney as steadily voted against slavery prohibition and against all compromises. By this, Mr. King showed that, in his understanding, no line dividing local from Federal authority, nor anything in the Constitution, was violated by Congress prohibiting slavery in Federal territory ; while Mr. Pinckney, by his votes, showed that, in his understanding, there was some sufficient reason for opposing such prohibition in that case.

The cases I have mentioned are the only acts of the "thirty-nine," or of any of them, upon the direct issue, which I have been able to discover.

To enumerate the persons who thus acted as being four in 1784, two in 1787, seventeen in 1789, three in 1798, two in 1804, and two in 1819–20, there would be thirty of them. But this would be counting John Langdon, Roger Sherman, William Few, Rufus King, and George Read each twice, and Abraham Baldwin three times. The true number of those of the "thirty-nine" whom I have shown to have acted upon the question which, by the text, they understood better than we, is twenty-three, leaving sixteen not shown to have acted upon it in any way.

Address at Cooper Institute

Here, then, we have twenty-three out of our thirty-nine fathers "who framed the government under which we live," who have, upon their official responsibility and their corporal oaths, acted upon the very question which the text affirms they "understood just as well, and even better, than we do now;" and twenty-one of them—a clear majority of the whole "thirty-nine"—so acting upon it as to make them guilty of gross political impropriety and wilful perjury if, in their understanding, any proper division between local and Federal authority, or anything in the Constitution they had made themselves, and sworn to support, forbade the Federal Government to control as to slavery in the Federal Territories. Thus the twenty-one acted; and, as actions speak louder than words, so actions under such responsibility speak still louder.

Two of the twenty-three voted against congressional prohibition of slavery in the Federal Territories, in the instances in which they acted upon the question. But for what reasons they so voted is not known. They may have done so because they thought a proper division of local from Federal authority, or some provision or principle of the Constitution, stood in the way; or they may, without any such question, have voted against the prohibition on what appeared to them to be sufficient grounds of expediency. No one who has sworn to support the Constitution can conscientiously vote for what he understands to be an unconstitutional measure, however expedient he may think it ; but one may and ought to vote against a measure which he deems constitutional if, at the same time, he deems it inexpedient. It, therefore, would be unsafe to set down even the two who voted against the prohibition as having done so because, in their understanding, any proper division of local from Federal authority, or anything in the Constitution, forbade the Federal Government to control as to slavery in Federal territory.

The remaining sixteen of the "thirty-nine," so far as I have discovered, have left no record of their understanding upon the direct question of Federal control of slavery in the Federal Territories. But there is much reason to believe that their understanding upon that question would not have appeared different from that of their twenty-three compeers, had it been manifested at all.

For the purpose of adhering rigidly to the text, I have purposely omitted whatever understanding may have been manifested by any person, however distinguished, other than the thirty-nine fathers who framed the original Constitution ; and, for the same reason, I have also omitted whatever understanding may have been manifested by any of the "thirty-nine" even on any other phase of the general question of slavery. If we should look into their acts and declarations on those other phases, as the foreign slave-trade, and the morality and policy of slavery generally, it would appear to us that on the direct question of Federal control of slavery in Federal Territories, the sixteen, if they had acted at all, would probably have acted just as the twenty-three did. Among that sixteen were several of the most noted anti-slavery men of those times—as Dr. Franklin, Alexander Hamilton, and Gouverneur Morris—while there was not one now known to have been otherwise, unless it may be John Rutledge, of South Carolina.

The sum of the whole is that of our thirty-nine fathers who framed the original Constitution, twenty-one—a clear majority of the whole —certainly understood that no proper division of local from Federal authority, nor any part of the Constitution, forbade the Federal Government to control slavery in the Federal Territories; while all the rest had probably the same understanding. Such, unquestionably, was the understanding of our fathers who framed the original Constitution; and the text affirms that they understood the question "better than we."

But, so far, I have been considering the understanding of the question manifested by the framers of the original Constitution. In and by the original instrument, a mode was provided for amending it; and, as I have already stated, the present frame of "the government under which we live" consists of that original, and twelve amendatory articles framed and adopted since. Those who now insist that Federal control of slavery in Federal Territories violates the Constitution, point us to the provisions which they suppose it thus violates; and, as I understand, they all fix upon provisions in these amendatory articles, and not in the original instrument. The Supreme Court, in the Dred Scott case, plant themselves upon the fifth amendment, which provides that no person shall be deprived of "life, liberty, or property without due process of law;" while Senator Douglas and his peculiar adherents plant themselves upon the tenth amendment, providing that "the powers not delegated to the United States by the Constitution" "are reserved to the States respectively, or to the people."

Now it so happens that these amendments were framed by the first Congress which sat under the Constitution—the identical Congress which passed the act, already mentioned, enforcing the prohibition of slavery in the Northwestern Territory. Not only was it the same Congress, but they were the identical, same individual men who, at the same session, and at the same time within the session, had under consideration, and in progress toward maturity, these constitutional amendments, and this act prohibiting slavery in all the territory the nation then owned. The constitutional amendments were introduced before, and passed after, the act enforcing the ordinance of '87 ; so that, during the whole pendency of the act to enforce the ordinance, the constitutional amendments were also pending.

The seventy-six members of that Congress, including sixteen of the framers of the original Constitution, as before stated, were pre-eminently our fathers who framed that part of "the government under which we live" which is now claimed as forbidding the Federal Government to control slavery in the Federal Territories.

Is it not a little presumptuous in any one at this day to affirm that the two things which that Congress deliberately framed, and carried to maturity at the same time, are absolutely inconsistent with each other? And does not such affirmation become impudently absurd when coupled with the other affirmation from the same mouth, that those who did the two things alleged to be inconsistent, understood whether they really were inconsistent better than we—better than he who affirms that they are inconsistent?

It is surely safe to assume that the thirty-nine framers of the original Constitution, and the seventy-six members of the Congress which framed the amendments thereto, taken together, do certainly include those who may be fairly called "our fathers who framed the government under which we live." And so assuming, I defy any man to show that any one of them ever, in his whole life, declared that, in his understanding, any proper division of local from Federal authority, or any part of the Constitution, forbade the Federal Government to control as to slavery in the Federal Territories. I go a step further. I defy any one to show that any living man in the whole world ever did, prior to the beginning of the present century (and I might almost say prior to the beginning of the last half of the present century), declare that, in his understanding, any proper division of local from Federal authority, or any part of the Constitution, forbade the Federal Government to control as to slavery in the Federal Territories. To those who now so declare I give not only "our fathers who framed the government under which we live," but with them all other living men within the century in which it was framed, among whom to search, and they shall not be able to find the evidence of a single man agreeing with them.

Now, and here, let me guard a little against being misunderstood. I do not mean to say we are bound to follow implicitly in whatever our fathers did. To do so would be to discard all the lights of current experience—to reject all progress, all improvement. What I do say is that if we would supplant the opinions and policy of our fathers in any case, we should do so upon evidence so conclusive, and argument so clear, that even their great authority, fairly considered and weighed, cannot stand; and most surely not in a case whereof we ourselves

HOME OF LINCOLN, SPRINGFIELD, ILL.

declare they understood the question better than we.

If any man at this day sincerely believes that a proper division of local from Federal authority, or any part of the Constitution, forbids the Federal Government to control as to slavery in the Federal Territories, he is right to say so, and to enforce his position by all truthful evidence and fair argument which he can. But he has no right to mislead others, who have less access to history, and less leisure to study it, into the false belief that "our fathers who framed the government under which we live" were of the same opinion—thus substituting falsehood and deception for truthful evidence and fair argument. If any man at this day sincerely believes "our fathers who framed the government under which we live" used and applied principles, in other cases, which ought to have led them to understand that a proper division of local from Federal authority, or some part of the Constitution, forbids the Federal Government to control as to slavery in the Federal Territories, he is right to say so. But he should, at the same time, brave the responsibility of declaring that, in his opinion, he understands their principles better than they did themselves; and especially should he not shirk that responsibility by asserting that they "understood the question just as well, and even better, than we do now."

But enough! Let all who believe that "our

fathers who framed the government under which we live understood this question just as well, and even better, than we do now," speak as they spoke, and act as they acted upon it. This is all Republicans ask—all Republicans desire—in relation to slavery. As those fathers marked it, so let it be again marked, as an evil not to be extended, but to be tolerated and protected only because of and so far as its actual presence among us makes that toleration and protection a necessity. Let all the guaranties those fathers gave it be not grudgingly, but fully and fairly, maintained. For this Republicans contend, and with this, so far as I know or believe, they will be content.

And now, if they would listen—as I suppose they will not—I would address a few words to the Southern people.

I would say to them : You consider yourselves a reasonable and a just people ; and I consider that in the general qualities of reason and justice you are not inferior to any other people. Still, when you speak of us Republicans, you do so only to denounce us as reptiles, or, at the best, as no better than outlaws. You will grant a hearing to pirates or murderers, but nothing like it to " Black Republicans." In all your contentions with one another, each of you deems an unconditional condemnation of " Black Republicanism" as the first thing to be attended to. Indeed, such condemnation of us seems to be an indispensable prerequisite--license, so to

speak—among you to be admitted or permitted
to speak at all. Now can you or not be prevailed upon to pause and to consider whether
this is quite just to us, or even to yourselves?
Bring forward your charges and specifications,
and then be patient long enough to hear us
deny or justify.

You say we are sectional. We deny it. That
makes an issue ; and the burden of proof is
upon you. You produce your proof ; and what
is it? Why, that our party has no existence in
your section—gets no votes in your section.
The fact is substantially true ; but does it prove
the issue? If it does, then in case we should,
without change of principle, begin to get votes
in your section, we should thereby cease to be
sectional. You cannot escape this conclusion ;
and yet, are you willing to abide by it? If you
are, you will probably soon find that we have
ceased to be sectional, for we shall get votes in
your section this very year. You will then begin to discover, as the truth plainly is, that
your proof does not touch the issue. The fact
that we get no votes in your section is a fact of
your making, and not of ours. And if there be
fault in that fact, that fault is primarily yours,
and remains so until you show that we repel
you by some wrong principle or practice. If
we do repel you by any wrong principle or practice, the fault is ours ; but this brings you to
where you ought to have started—to a discussion of the right or wrong of our principle. If

our principle, put in practice, would wrong your section for the benefit of ours, or for any other object, then our principle, and we with it, are sectional, and are justly opposed and denounced as such. Meet us, then, on the question of whether our principle, put in practice, would wrong your section ; and so meet us as if it were possible that something may be said on our side. Do you accept the challenge ? No ! Then you really believe that the principle which "our fathers who framed the government under which we live" thought so clearly right as to adopt it, and indorse it again and again, upon their official oaths, is in fact so clearly wrong as to demand your condemnation without a moment's consideration.

Some of you delight to flaunt in our faces the warning against sectional parties given by Washington in his Farewell Address. Less than eight years before Washington gave that warning, he had, as President of the United States, approved and signed an act of Congress enforcing the prohibition of slavery in the Northwestern Territory, which act embodied the policy of the government upon that subject up to and at the very moment he penned that warning ; and about one year after he penned it, he wrote Lafayette that he considered that prohibition a wise measure, expressing in the same connection his hope that we should at some time have a confederacy of free States.

Bearing this in mind, and seeing that sectionalism has since arisen upon this same subject, is that warning a weapon in your hands against us, or in our hands against you? Could Washington himself speak, would he cast the blame of that sectionalism upon us, who sustain his policy, or upon you, who repudiate it? We respect that warning of Washington, and we commend it to you, together with his example pointing to the right application of it.

But you say you are conservative—eminently conservative—while we are revolutionary, destructive, or something of the sort. What is conservatism? Is it not adherence to the old and tried, against the new and untried? We stick to, contend for, the identical old policy on the point in controversy which was adopted by "our fathers who framed the government under which we live;" while you with one accord reject, and scout, and spit upon that old policy, and insist upon substituting something new. True, you disagree among yourselves as to what that substitute shall be. You are divided on new propositions and plans, but you are unanimous in rejecting and denouncing the old policy of the fathers. Some of you are for reviving the foreign slave-trade; some for a congressional slave code for the Territories; some for Congress forbidding the Territories to prohibit slavery within their limits; some for maintaining slavery in the Territories through the judiciary; some for the "gur-reat pur-rinciple" that "if one man would enslave another, no third man should object," fantastically called " popular sovereignty ;" but never a man among you is in favor of Federal prohibition of slavery in Federal Territories, according to the practice of " our fathers who framed the government under which we live." Not one of all your various plans can show a precedent or an advocate in the century within which our government originated. Consider, then, whether your claim of conservatism for yourselves, and your charge of destructiveness against us, are based on the most clear and stable foundations.

Again, you say we have made the slavery question more prominent than it formerly was. We deny it. We admit that it is more prominent, but we deny that we made it so. It was not we, but you, who discarded the old policy of the fathers. We resisted, and still resist, your innovation ; and thence comes the greater prominence of the question. Would you have that question reduced to its former proportions ? Go back to that old policy. What has been will be again, under the same conditions. If you would have the peace of the old times, re-adopt the precepts and policy of the old times.

You charge that we stir up insurrections among your slaves. We deny it ; and what is your proof? Harper's Ferry ! John Brown ! ! John Brown was no Republican ; and you have failed to implicate a single Republican in his Harper's Ferry enterprise. If any member of our party is guilty in that matter, you know it, or you do not know it. If you do know it, you are inexcusable for not designating the man and proving the fact. If you do not know it, you are inexcusable for asserting it, and especially for persisting in the assertion after you have tried and failed to make the proof. You need not be told that persisting in a charge which one does not know to be true, is simply malicious slander.

Some of you admit that no Republican designedly aided or encouraged the Harper's Ferry affair, but still insist that our doctrines and declarations necessarily lead to such results. We do not believe it. We know we hold no doctrine, and make no declaration, which were not held to and made by "our fathers who framed the government under which we live." You never dealt fairly by us in relation to this affair. When it occurred, some important State elections were near at hand, and you were in evident glee with the belief that, by charging the blame upon us, you could get an advantage of us in those elections. The elections came, and your expectations were not quite fulfilled. Every Republican man knew that, as to himself at least, your charge was a slander, and he was not much inclined by it to cast his vote in your favor. Republican doctrines and declarations are accompanied with a continual protest against any interference whatever with your slaves, or with you about your slaves. Surely, this does not encourage them to revolt. True, we do, in common with " our fathers who framed the government under which we live," declare our belief that slavery is wrong ; but the slaves do not hear us declare even this. For anything we say or do, the slaves would scarcely know there is a Republican party. I believe they would not, in fact, generally know it but for your misrepresentations of us in their hearing. In your political contests among yourselves, each faction charges the other with sympathy with Black Republicanism ; and then, to give point to the charge, defines Black Republicanism to simply be insurrection, blood, and thunder among the slaves.

Slave insurrections are no more common now than they were before the Republican party was organized. What induced the Southampton insurrection, twenty-eight years ago, in which at least three times as many lives were lost as at Harper's Ferry ? You can scarcely stretch your very elastic fancy to the conclusion that Southampton was " got up by Black Republicanism." In the present state of things in the United States, I do not think a general, or even a very extensive, slave insurrection is possible. The indispensable concert of action cannot be attained. The slaves have no means of rapid communication ; nor can incendiary freemen, black or white, supply it. The explosive materials are everywhere in parcels ; but there neither are, nor can be supplied, the indispensable connecting trains.

Much is said by Southern people about the affection of slaves for their masters and mistresses ; and a part of it, at least, is true. A plot for an uprising could scarcely be devised and communicated to twenty individuals before some one of them, to save the life of a favorite master or mistress, would divulge it. This is the rule ; and the slave revolution in Hayti was not an exception to it, but a case occurring under peculiar circumstances. The gunpowder plot of British history, though not connected with slaves, was more in point. In that case, only about twenty were admitted to the secret ; and yet one of them, in his anxiety to save a friend, betrayed the plot to that friend, and, by consequence, averted the calamity. Occasional poisonings from the kitchen, and open or stealthy assassinations in the field, and local revolts extending to a score or so, will continue to occur as the natural results of slavery ; but no general insurrection of slaves, as I think, can happen in this country for a long time. Whoever much fears, or much hopes, for such an event, will be alike disappointed.

In the language of Mr. Jefferson, uttered many years ago, " It is still in our power to direct the process of emancipation and deportation peaceably, and in such slow degrees, as that the evil will wear off insensibly ; and their places be, *pari passu*, filled up by free white laborers. If, on the contrary, it is left to force itself on, human nature must shudder at the prospect held up."

Mr. Jefferson did not mean to say, nor do I, that the power of emancipation is in the Federal Government. He spoke of Virginia ; and, as to the power of emancipation, I speak of the slaveholding States only. The Federal Government, however, as we insist, has the power of restraining the extension of the institution—the power to insure that a slave insurrection shall never occur on any American soil which is now free from slavery.

John Brown's effort was peculiar. It was not a slave insurrection. It was an attempt by white men to get up a revolt among slaves, in which the slaves refused to participate. In fact, it was so absurd that the slaves, with all their ignorance, saw plainly enough it could not succeed. That affair, in its philosophy, corresponds with the many attempts, related in history, at the assassination of kings and emperors. An enthusiast broods over the oppression of a people till he fancies himself commissioned by Heaven to liberate them. He ventures the attempt, which ends in little else than his own execution. Orsini's attempt on Louis Napoleon, and John Brown's attempt at Harper's Ferry, were, in their philosophy, precisely the same. The eagerness to cast blame on old England in the one case, and on New

England in the other, does not disprove the sameness of the two things.

And how much would it avail you, if you could, by the use of John Brown, Helper's Book, and the like, break up the Republican organization? Human action can be modified to some extent, but human nature cannot be changed. There is a judgment and a feeling against slavery in this nation, which cast at least a million and a half of votes. You cannot destroy that judgment and feeling—that sentiment—by breaking up the political organization which rallies around it. You can scarcely scatter and disperse an army which has been formed into order in the face of your heaviest fire ; but if you could, how much would you gain by forcing the sentiment which created it out of the peaceful channel of the ballot-box into some other channel? What would that other channel probably be? Would the number of John Browns be lessened or enlarged by the operation?

But you will break up the Union rather than submit to a denial of your constitutional rights.

That has a somewhat reckless sound ; but it would be palliated, if not fully justified, were we proposing, by the mere force of numbers, to deprive you of some right plainly written down in the Constitution. But we are proposing no such thing.

When you make these declarations you have

a specific and well-understood allusion to an assumed constitutional right of yours to take slaves into the Federal Territories, and to hold them there as property. But no such right is specially written in the Constitution. That instrument is literally silent about any such right. We, on the contrary, deny that such a right has any existence in the Constitution, even by implication.

Your purpose, then, plainly stated, is that you will destroy the government, unless you be allowed to construe and force the Constitution as you please, on all points in dispute between you and us. You will rule or ruin in all events.

This, plainly stated, is your language. Perhaps you will say the Supreme Court has decided the disputed constitutional question in your favor. Not quite so. But waiving the lawyer's distinction between dictum and decision, the court has decided the question for you in a sort of way. The court has substantially said, it is your constitutional right to take slaves into the Federal Territories, and to hold them there as property. When I say the decision was made in a sort of way, I mean it was made in a divided court, by a bare majority of the judges, and they not quite agreeing with one another in the reasons for making it ; that it is so made as that its avowed supporters disagree with one another about its meaning, and that it was mainly based upon a mistaken statement of fact—the statement in the opinion that "the right of property in a slave is distinctly and expressly affirmed in the Constitution."

An inspection of the Constitution will show that the right of property in a slave is not "distinctly and expressly affirmed" in it. Bear in mind, the judges do not pledge their judicial opinion that such right is impliedly affirmed in the Constitution ; but they pledge their veracity that it is "distinctly and expressly" affirmed there—"distinctly," that is, not mingled with anything else—"expressly," that is, in words meaning just that, without the aid of any inference, and susceptible of no other meaning.

If they had only pledged their judicial opinion that such right is affirmed in the instrument by implication, it would be open to others to show that neither the word "slave" nor "slavery" is to be found in the Constitution, nor the word "property" even, in any connection with language alluding to the thing slave, or slavery ; and that wherever in that instrument the slave is alluded to, he is called a "person ;" and wherever his master's legal right in relation to him is alluded to, it is spoken of as "service or labor which may be due"—as a debt payable in service or labor. Also it would be open to show, by contemporaneous history, that this mode of alluding to slaves and slavery, instead of speaking of them, was employed on purpose to exclude from the Constitution the idea that there could be property in man.

To show all this is easy and certain.

When this obvious mistake of the judges shall be brought to their notice, is it not reasonable to expect that they will withdraw the mistaken statement, and reconsider the conclusion based upon it ?

And then it is to be remembered that '' our fathers who framed the government under which we live''—the men who made the Constitution—decided this same constitutional question in our favor long ago : decided it without division among themselves when making the decision ; without division among themselves about the meaning of it after it was made, and, so far as any evidence is left, without basing it upon any mistaken statement of facts.

Under all these circumstances, do you really feel yourselves justified to break up this government unless such a court decision as yours is shall be at once submitted to as a conclusive and final rule of political action ? But you will not abide the election of a Republican president ! In that supposed event, you say, you will destroy the Union ; and then, you say, the great crime of having destroyed it will be upon us ! That is cool. A highwayman holds a pistol to my ear, and mutters through his teeth, '' Stand and deliver, or I shall kill you, and then you will be a murderer !''

To be sure, what the robber demanded of me—my money—was my own ; and I had a clear right to keep it ; but it was no more my own than my vote is my own ; and the threat of death to me, to extort my money, and the threat of destruction to the Union, to extort my vote, can scarcely be distinguished in principle.

A few words now to Republicans. It is exceedingly desirable that all parts of this great Confederacy shall be at peace, and in harmony one with another. Let us Republicans do our part to have it so. Even though much provoked, let us do nothing through passion and ill temper. Even though the Southern people will not so much as listen to us, let us calmly consider their demands, and yield to them if, in our deliberate view of our duty, we possibly can. Judging by all they say and do, and by the subject and nature of their controversy with us, let us determine, if we can, what will satisfy them.

Will they be satisfied if the Territories be unconditionally surrendered to them ? We know they will not. In all their present complaints against us, the Territories are scarcely mentioned. Invasions and insurrections are the rage now. Will it satisfy them if, in the future, we have nothing to do with invasions and insurrections? We know it will not. We so know, because we know we never had anything to do with invasions and insurrections ; and yet this total abstaining does not exempt us from the charge and the denunciation.

The question recurs, What will satisfy them ? Simply this : we must not only let them alone, but we must somehow convince them that we do let them alone. This, we know by experience, is no easy task. We have been so trying to convince them from the very beginning of our organization, but with no success. In all our platforms and speeches we have constantly protested our purpose to let them alone; but this has had no tendency to convince them. Alike unavailing to convince them is the fact that they have never detected a man of us in any attempt to disturb them.

These natural and apparently adequate means all failing, what will convince them? This, and this only: cease to call slavery wrong, and join them in calling it right. And this must be done thoroughly—done in acts as well as in words. Silence will not be tolerated—we must place ourselves avowedly with them. Senator Douglas's new sedition law must be enacted and enforced, suppressing all declarations that slavery is wrong, whether made in politics, in presses, in pulpits, or in private. We must arrest and return their fugitive slaves with greedy pleasure. We must pull down our free-State constitutions. The whole atmosphere must be disinfected from all taint of opposition to slavery, before they will cease to believe that all their troubles proceed from us.

I am quite aware they do not state their case precisely in this way. Most of them would probably say to us, "Let us alone; do nothing to us, and say what you please about slavery."

Address at Cooper Institute

But we do let them alone—have never disturbed them—so that, after all, it is what we say which dissatisfies them. They will continue to accuse us of doing, until we cease saying.

I am also aware they have not as yet in terms demanded the overthrow of our free-State constitutions. Yet those constitutions declare the wrong of slavery with more solemn emphasis than do all other sayings against it ; and when all these other sayings shall have been silenced, the overthrow of these constitutions will be demanded, and nothing be left to resist the demand. It is nothing to the contrary that they do not demand the whole of this just now. Demanding what they do, and for the reason they do, they can voluntarily stop nowhere short of this consummation. Holding, as they do, that slavery is morally right and socially elevating, they cannot cease to demand a full national recognition of it as a legal right and a social blessing.

Nor can we justifiably withhold this on any ground save our conviction that slavery is wrong. If slavery is right, all words, acts, laws, and constitutions against it are themselves wrong, and should be silenced and swept away. If it is right, we cannot justly object to its nationality—its universality ; if it is wrong, they cannot justly insist upon its extension—its enlargement. All they ask we could readily grant, if we thought slavery right ; all we ask they could as readily grant, if they thought it

wrong. Their thinking it right and our thinking it wrong is the precise fact upon which depends the whole controversy. Thinking it
right, as they do, they are not to blame for de-
siring its full recognition as being right; but
thinking it wrong, as we do, can we yield to
them? Can we cast our votes with their view,
and against our own? In view of our moral,
social, and political responsibilities, can we do
this?

Wrong as we think slavery is, we can yet
afford to let it alone where it is, because that
much is due to the necessity arising from its
actual presence in the nation; but can we,
while our votes will prevent it, allow it to
spread into the national Territories, and to
overrun us here in these free States? If our
sense of duty forbids this, then let us stand by
our duty fearlessly and effectively. Let us be
diverted by none of those sophistical contrivances wherewith we are so industriously plied
and belabored—contrivances such as groping
for some middle ground between the right and
the wrong: vain as the search for a man who
should be neither a living man nor a dead
man; such as a policy of "don't care" on a
question about which all true men do care;
such as Union appeals beseeching true Union
men to yield to Disunionists, reversing the
divine rule, and calling, not the sinners, but
the righteous to repentance; such as invoca-
tions to Washington, imploring men to unsay

what Washington said and undo what Washington did.

Neither let us be slandered from our duty by false accusations against us, nor frightened from it by menaces of destruction to the government, nor of dungeons to ourselves. Let us have faith that right makes might, and in that faith let us to the end dare to do our duty as we understand it.

Farewell at Springfield

February 11, 1861

[These words, to which subsequent events have given an added note of solemnity, were spoken to a vast audience of Lincoln's fellow-citizens upon the rainy February day when he left Springfield for Washington to assume the duties of the Presidency.]

My Friends: No one, not in my situation, can appreciate my feeling of sadness at this parting. To this place, and the kindness of these people, I owe everything. Here I have lived a quarter of a century, and have passed from a young to an old man. Here my children have been born, and one is buried. I now leave, not knowing when or whether ever I may return, with a task before me greater than that which rested upon Washington. Without the assistance of that Divine Being who ever attended him, I cannot succeed. With that assistance, I cannot fail. Trusting in Him who can go with me, and remain with you, and be everywhere for good, let us confidently hope that all will yet be well. To His care commending you, as I hope in your prayers you will commend me, I bid you an affectionate farewell.

Speech in Independence **Hall**, Philadelphia

February 22, 1861

[During the journey to Washington **Lincoln** made many brief addresses. The following, spoken in Independence Hall, Philadelphia, upon Washington's Birthday, is one of the most felicitous, and the time and place of its delivery give it additional interest.]

Mr. Cuyler : I am filled with deep emotion at finding myself standing in this place, where were collected together the wisdom, the patriotism, the devotion to principle, from which sprang the institutions under which we live. You have kindly suggested to me that in my hands is the task of restoring peace to our distracted country. I can say in return, sir, that all the political sentiments I entertain have been drawn, so far as I have been able to draw them, from the sentiments which originated in and were given to the world from this hall. I have never had a feeling, politically, that did not spring from the sentiments embodied in the Declaration of Independence. I have often pondered over the dangers which were incurred by the men who assembled here and framed and adopted that Declaration. I have pondered over the toils that were endured by the officers and soldiers of the army who achieved that independence. I have often inquired of myself what great principle or idea it was that kept this Confederacy so long together. It was not the mere matter of separation of the colonies from the motherland, but that sentiment in the Declaration of Independence which gave liberty not alone to the people of this country, but hope to all the world, for all future time. It was that which gave promise that in due time the weights would be lifted from the shoulders of all men, and that all should have an equal chance. This is the sentiment embodied in the Declaration of Independence. Now, my friends, can this country be saved on that basis? If it can, I will consider myself one of the happiest men in the world if I can help to save it. If it cannot be saved upon that principle, it will be truly awful. But if this country cannot be saved without giving up that principle, I was about to say I would rather be assassinated on this spot than surrender it. Now, in my view of the present aspect of affairs, there is no need of bloodshed and war. There is no necessity for it. I am not in favor of such a course ; and I may say in advance that there will be no bloodshed unless it is forced upon the government. The government will not use force, unless force is used against it.

My friends, this is wholly an unprepared

speech. I did not expect to be called on to say
a word when I came here. I supposed I was
merely to do something toward raising a flag.
I may, therefore, have said something indis-
creet. [Cries of " No, no."] But I have said
nothing but what I am willing to live by, and,
if it be the pleasure of Almighty God, to die by.

First Inaugural Address.

March 4, 1861.

["Mr. Lincoln was simply introduced by Senator Baker, of Oregon, and delivered his inaugural address. His voice had great carrying capacity, and the vast crowd heard with ease a speech of which every sentence was fraught with an importance and scrutinized with an anxiety far beyond that of any other speech ever delivered in the United States. . . . The inaugural address was simple, earnest, and direct, unincumbered by that rhetorical ornamentation which the American people have always admired as the highest form of eloquence. Those Northerners who had expected magniloquent periods and exaggerated outbursts of patriotism were disappointed, and as they listened in vain for the scream of the eagle, many grumbled at the absence of what they conceived to be *force*. Yet the general feeling was of satisfaction, which grew as the address was more thoroughly studied." — *Morse's "Abraham Lincoln."*]

Fellow-citizens of the United States: In compliance with a custom as old as the government itself, I appear before you to address you briefly, and to take in your presence the oath prescribed by the Constitution of the United States to be taken by the President "before he enters on the execution of his office."

74

First Inaugural Address

I do not consider it necessary at present for me to discuss those matters of administration about which there is no special anxiety or excitement.

Apprehension seems to exist among the people of the Southern States that by the accession of a Republican administration their property and their peace and personal security are to be endangered. There has never been any reasonable cause for such apprehension. Indeed, the most ample evidence to the contrary has all the while existed and been open to their inspection. It is found in nearly all the published speeches of him who now addresses you. I do but quote from one of those speeches when I declare that " I have no purpose, directly or indirectly, to interfere with the institution of slavery in the States where it exists. I believe I have no lawful right to do so, and I have no inclination to do so." Those who nominated and elected me did so with full knowledge that I had made this and many similar declarations, and had never recanted them. And, more than this, they placed in the platform for my acceptance, and as a law to themselves and to me, the clear and emphatic resolution which I now read :

" *Resolved*, That the maintenance inviolate of the rights of the States, and especially the right of each State to order and control its own domestic institutions according to its own judgment exclusively, is essential to that balance of power on which the perfection and endurance of our political fabric depend, and we denounce the lawless invasion by armed force of the soil of any State or Territory, no matter under what pretext, as among the gravest of crimes.''

I now reiterate these sentiments; and, in doing so, I only press upon the public attention the most conclusive evidence of which the case is susceptible, that the property, peace, and security of no section are to be in any wise endangered by the now incoming administration. I add, too, that all the protection which, consistently with the Constitution and the laws, can be given, will be cheerfully given to all the States when lawfully demanded, for whatever cause—as cheerfully to one section as to another.

There is much controversy about the delivering up of fugitives from service or labor. The clause I now read is as plainly written in the Constitution as any other of its provisions:

'' No person held to service or labor in one State, under the laws thereof, escaping into another, shall in consequence of any law or regulation therein be discharged from such service or labor, but shall be delivered up on claim of the party to whom such service or labor may be due.''

It is scarcely questioned that this provision was intended by those who made it for the reclaiming of what we call fugitive slaves; and the intention of the lawgiver is the law. All members of Congress swear their support to the whole Constitution—to this provision as much as to any other. To the proposition, then, that slaves whose cases come within the terms of this clause " shall be delivered up," their oaths are unanimous. Now, if they would make the effort in good temper, could they not with nearly equal unanimity frame and pass a law by means of which to keep good that unanimous oath ?

There is some difference of opinion whether this clause should be enforced by national or by State authority ; but surely that difference is not a very material one. If the slave is to be surrendered, it can be of but little consequence to him or to others by which authority it is done. And should any one in any case be content that his oath shall go unkept on a merely unsubstantial controversy as to how it shall be kept ?

Again, in any law upon this subject, ought not all the safeguards of liberty known in civilized and humane jurisprudence to be introduced, so that a free man be not, in any case, surrendered as a slave ? And might it not be well at the same time to provide by law for the enforcement of that clause in the Constitution which guarantees that " the citizen of each State shall be entitled to all privileges and immunities of citizens in the several States" ?

I take the official oath to-day with no mental reservations, and with no purpose to construe the Constitution or laws by any hypercritical rules. And while I do not choose now to specify

particular acts of Congress as proper to be enforced, I do suggest that it will be much safer
for all, both in official and private stations, to
conform to and abide by all those acts which
stand unrepealed, than to violate any of them,
trusting to find impunity in having them held
to be unconstitutional.

It is seventy-two years since the first inauguration of a President under our National Constitution. During that period fifteen different
and greatly distinguished citizens have, in succession, administered the executive branch of
the government. They have conducted it
through many perils, and generally with great
success. Yet, with all this scope of precedent,
I now enter upon the same task for the brief
constitutional term of four years under great
and peculiar difficulty. A disruption of the
Federal Union, heretofore only menaced, is
now formidably attempted.

I hold that, in contemplation of universal law
and of the Constitution, the Union of these
States is perpetual. Perpetuity is implied, if
not expressed, in the fundamental law of all
national governments. It is safe to assert that
no government proper ever had a provision in
its organic law for its own termination. Continue to execute all the express provisions of
our National Constitution, and the Union will
endure forever—it being impossible to destroy
it except by some action not provided for in the
instrument itself.

First Inaugural Address

Again, if the United States be not a government proper, but an association of States in the nature of contract merely, can it, as a contract, be peaceably unmade by less than all the parties who made it? One party to a contract may violate it—break it, so to speak ; but does it not require all to lawfully rescind it?

Descending from these general principles, we find the proposition that, in legal contemplation the Union is perpetual confirmed by the history of the Union itself. The Union is much older than the Constitution. It was formed, in fact, by the Articles of Association in 1774. It was matured and continued by the Declaration of Independence in 1776. It was further matured, and the faith of all the then thirteen States expressly plighted and engaged that it should be perpetual, by the Articles of Confederation in 1778. And, finally, in 1787 one of the declared objects for ordaining and establishing the Constitution was " to form a more perfect Union."

But if the destruction of the Union by one or by a part only of the States be lawfully possible, the Union is less perfect than before the Constitution, having lost the vital element of perpetuity.

It follows from these views that no State upon its own mere motion can lawfully get out of the Union ; that resolves and ordinances to that effect are legally void ; and that acts of violence. within any State or States, against the

authority of the United States, are insurrection-
ary or revolutionary, according to circumstances.

I therefore consider that, in view of the Constitution and the laws, the Union is unbroken;
and to the extent of my ability I shall take care,
as the Constitution itself expressly enjoins upon
me, that the laws of the Union be faithfully
executed in all the States. Doing this I deem
to be only a simple duty on my part; and I
shall perform it so far as practicable, unless my
rightful masters, the American people, shall
withhold the requisite means, or in some au-
thoritative manner direct the contrary. I trust
this will not be regarded as a menace, but only
as the declared purpose of the Union that it
will constitutionally defend and maintain itself.

In doing this there needs to be no bloodshed
or violence; and there shall be none, unless it
be forced upon the national authority. The
power confided to me will be used to hold, occupy, and possess the property and places be-
longing to the government, and to collect the
duties and imposts; but beyond what may be
necessary for these objects, there will be no invasion, no using of force against or among the
people anywhere. Where hostility to the
United States, in any interior locality, shall be
so great and universal as to prevent competent
resident citizens from holding the Federal
offices, there will be no attempt to force obnoxious strangers among the people for that object.

First Inaugural Address

While the strict legal right may exist in the government to enforce the exercise of these offices, the attempt to do so would be so irritating, and so nearly impracticable withal, that I deem it better to forego for the time the uses of such offices.

The mails, unless repelled, will continue to be furnished in all parts of the Union. So far as possible, the people everywhere shall have that sense of perfect security which is most favorable to calm thought and reflection. The course here indicated will be followed unless current events and experience shall show a modification or change to be proper, and in every case and exigency my best discretion will be exercised according to circumstances actually existing, and with a view and a hope of a peaceful solution of the national troubles and the restoration of fraternal sympathies and affections.

That there are persons in one section or another who seek to destroy the Union at all events, and are glad of any pretext to do it, I will neither affirm nor deny ; but if there be such, I need address no word to them. To those, however, who really love the Union may I not speak ?

Before entering upon so grave a matter as the destruction of our national fabric, with all its benefits, its memories, and its hopes, would it not be wise to ascertain precisely why we do it ? Will you hazard so desperate a step while there is any possibility that any portion of the ills you fly from have no real existence? Will you, while the certain ills you fly to are greater than all the real ones you fly from—will you risk the commission of so fearful a mistake?

All profess to be content in the Union if all constitutional rights can be maintained. Is it true, then, that any right, plainly written in the Constitution, has been denied? I think not. Happily the human mind is so constituted that no party can reach to the audacity of doing this. Think, if you can, of a single instance in which a plainly written provision of the Constitution has ever been denied. If by the mere force of numbers a majority should deprive a minority of any clearly written constitutional right, it might, in a moral point of view, justify revolution—certainly would if such a right were a vital one. But such is not our case. All the vital rights of minorities and of individuals are so plainly assured to them by affirmations and negations, guarantees and prohibitions, in the Constitution, that controversies never arise concerning them. But no organic law can ever be framed with a provision specifically applicable to every question which may occur in practical administration. No foresight can anticipate, nor any document of reasonable length contain, express provisions for all possible questions. Shall fugitives from labor be surrendered by national or by State authority? The Constitution does not expressly say. *May* Congress prohibit slavery in the Territories? The Constitution does not expressly say. *Must* Congress protect slavery in the Territories? The Constitution does not expressly say.

From questions of this class spring all our constitutional controversies, and we divide upon them into majorities and minorities. If the minority will not acquiesce, the majority must, or the government must cease. There is no other alternative ; for continuing the government is acquiescence on one side or the other.

If a minority in such case will secede rather than acquiesce, they make a precedent which in turn will divide and ruin them ; for a minority of their own will secede from them whenever a majority refuses to be controlled by such minority. For instance, why may not any portion of a new confederacy a year or two hence arbitrarily secede again, precisely as portions of the present Union now claim to secede from it? All who cherish disunion sentiments are now being educated to the exact temper of doing this.

Is there such perfect identity of interests among the States to compose a new Union, as to produce harmony only, and prevent renewed secession ?

Plainly, the central idea of secession is the essence of anarchy. A majority held in restraint by constitutional checks and limitations, and always changing easily with deliberate changes of popular opinions and sentiments, is the only true sovereign of a free people. Whoever rejects it does, of necessity, fly to anarchy or to despotism. Unanimity is impossible ; the rule of a minority, as a permanent arrangement, is wholly inadmissible ; so that, rejecting the majority principle, anarchy or despotism in some form is all that is left.

I do not forget the position, assumed by some, that constitutional questions are to be decided by the Supreme Court ; nor do I deny that such decisions must be binding, in any case, upon the parties to a suit, as to the object of that suit, while they are also entitled to very high respect and consideration in all parallel cases by all other departments of the government. And while it is obviously possible that such decision may be erroneous in any given case, still the evil effect following it, being limited to that particular case, with the chance that it may be overruled and never become a precedent for other cases, can better be borne than could the evils of a different practice. At the same time, the candid citizen must confess that if the policy of the government, upon vital questions affecting the whole people, is to be irrevocably fixed by decisions of the Supreme Court, the instant they are made, in ordinary litigation between parties in personal actions, the people will have ceased to be their own rulers, having to that extent practically resigned their government into the hands of that eminent tribunal. Nor is there in this view any assault upon the court or the judges. It is a duty from which they may not shrink to decide cases properly brought before them, and it is no fault of theirs if others seek to turn their decisions to political purposes.

One section of our country believes slavery is right, and ought to be extended, while the other believes it is wrong, and ought not to be extended. This is the only substantial dispute. The fugitive-slave clause of the Constitution, and the law for the suppression of the foreign slave-trade, are each as well enforced, perhaps, as any law can ever be in a community where the moral sense of the people imperfectly supports the law itself. The great body of the people abide by the dry legal obligation in both cases, and a few break over in each. This, I think, cannot be perfectly cured ; and it would be worse in both cases after the separation of the sections than before. The foreign slave-trade, now imperfectly suppressed, would be ultimately revived, without restriction, in one section, while fugitive slaves, now only partially surrendered, would not be surrendered at all by the other.

Physically speaking, we cannot separate. We cannot remove our respective sections from each other, nor build an impassable wall between them. A husband and wife may be divorced, and go out of the presence and beyond the reach of each other ; but the different parts of our country cannot do this. They cannot but remain face to face, and intercourse, either amicable or hostile, must continue between them. Is it possible, then, to make that intercourse more advantageous or more satisfactory after separation than before? Can aliens make treaties easier than friends can make laws? Can treaties be more faithfully enforced between aliens than laws can among friends? Suppose you go to war, you cannot fight always; and when, after much loss on both sides, and no gain on either, you cease fighting, the identical old questions as to terms of intercourse are again upon you.

This country, with its institutions, belongs to the people who inhabit it. Whenever they shall grow weary of the existing government, they can exercise their constitutional right of amending it, or their revolutionary right to dismember or overthrow it. I cannot be ignorant of the fact that many worthy and patriotic citizens are desirous of having the National Constitution amended. While I make no recommendation of amendments, I fully recognize the rightful authority of the people over the whole subject, to be exercised in either of the modes prescribed in the instrument itself; and I should, under existing circumstances, favor rather than oppose a fair opportunity being afforded the people to act upon it. I will venture to add that to me the convention mode seems preferable, in that it allows amendments to originate with the people themselves, instead of only permitting them to take or reject propositions originated by others not especially chosen for the purpose, and which might not be precisely such as they would wish to either accept or refuse. I understand a proposed amendment to the Constitution—which amendment, however, I have not seen—has passed Congress, to the effect that the Federal Government shall never interfere with the domestic institutions of the States, including that of persons held to service. To avoid misconstruction of what I have said, I depart from my purpose not to speak of particular amendments so far as to say that, holding such a provision to now be implied constitutional law, I have no objection to its being made express and irrevocable.

The chief magistrate derives all his authority from the people, and they have conferred none upon him to fix terms for the separation of the States. The people themselves can do this also if they choose ; but the executive, as such, has nothing to do with it. His duty is to administer the present government, as it came to his hands, and to transmit it, unimpaired by him, to his successor.

Why should there not be a patient confidence in the ultimate justice of the people ? Is there any better or equal hope in the world ? In our present differences is either party without faith of being in the right ? If the Almighty Ruler of Nations, with his eternal truth and justice, be on your side of the North, or on yours of the South, that truth and that justice will surely prevail by the judgment of this great tribunal of the American people.

By the frame of the government under which we live, this same people have wisely given their public servants but little power for mischief ; and have, with equal wisdom, provided for the return of that little to their own hands at very short intervals. While the people retain their virtue and vigilance, no administration, by any extreme of wickedness or folly, can very seriously injure the government in the short space of four years.

My countrymen, one and all, think calmly and well upon this whole subject. Nothing valuable can be lost by taking time. If there be an object to hurry any of you in hot haste to a step which you would never take deliberately, that object will be frustrated by taking time ; but no good object can be frustrated by it. Such of you as are now dissatisfied, still have the old Constitution unimpaired, and, on the sensitive point, the laws of your own framing under it ; while the new administration will have no immediate power, if it would, to change either. If it were admitted that you who are dissatisfied hold the right side in the dispute, there still is no single good reason for precipitate action. Intelligence, patriotism, Christianity, and a firm reliance on Him who has never yet forsaken this favored land, are still competent to adjust in the best way all our present difficulty.

First Inaugural Address

In your hands, my dissatisfied fellow-countrymen, and not in mine, is the momentous issue of civil war. The government will not assail you. You can have no conflict without being yourselves the aggressors. You have no oath registered in heaven to destroy the government, while I shall have the most solemn one to " preserve, protect, and defend it."

I am loath to close. We are not enemies, but friends. We must not be enemies. Though passion may have strained, it must not break our bonds of affection. The mystic chords of memory, stretching from every battle-field and patriot grave to every living heart and hearthstone all over this broad land, will yet swell the chorus of the Union when again touched, as surely they will be, by the better angels of our nature.

Emancipation Proclamation

January 1, 1863

BY THE PRESIDENT OF THE UNITED STATES OF
AMERICA :

A Proclamation

Whereas, on the twenty-second day of September, in the year of our Lord one thousand eight hundred and sixty-two, a proclamation was issued by the President of the United States, containing, among other things, the following, to wit :

" That on the first day of January, in the year of our Lord one thousand eight hundred and sixty-three, all persons held as slaves within any State, or designated part of a State, the people whereof shall then be in rebellion against the United States, shall be then, thenceforward, and forever free ; and the Executive Government of the United States, including the military and naval authority thereof, will recognize and maintain the freedom of such persons, and will do no act or acts to repress such persons, or any of them, in any efforts they may make for their actual freedom.

" That the Executive will, on the first day of

Emancipation Proclamation

January aforesaid, by proclamation, designate the States and parts of States, if any, in which the people thereof respectively shall then be in rebellion against the United States; and the fact that any State, or the people thereof, shall on that day be in good faith represented in the Congress of the United States by members chosen thereto at elections wherein a majority of the qualified voters of such State shall have participated, shall in the absence of strong countervailing testimony be deemed conclusive evidence that such State and the people thereof are not then in rebellion against the United States."

Now, therefore, I, Abraham Lincoln, President of the United States, by virtue of the power in me vested as commander-in-chief of the army and navy of the United States, in time of actual armed rebellion against the authority and government of the United States, and as a fit and necessary war measure for suppressing said rebellion, do, on this first day of January, in the year of our Lord one thousand eight hundred and sixty-three, and in accordance with my purpose so to do, publicly proclaimed for the full period of 100 days from the day first above mentioned, order and designate as the States and parts of States wherein the people thereof, respectively, are this day in rebellion against the United States, the following, to wit:

Arkansas, Texas, Louisiana (except the par-

ishes of St. Bernard, Plaquemines, Jefferson,
St. John, St. Charles, St. James, Ascension,
Assumption, Terre Bonne, Lafourche, St. Mary,
St. Martin, and Orleans, including the city of
New Orleans), Mississippi, Alabama, Florida,
Georgia, South Carolina, North Carolina, and
Virginia (except the forty-eight counties desig-
nated as West Virginia, and also the counties
of Berkeley, Accomac, Northampton, Elizabeth
City, York, Princess Ann, and Norfolk, includ-
ing the cities of Norfolk and Portsmouth), and
which excepted parts are for the present left
precisely as if this proclamation were not
issued.

And by virtue of the power and for the purpose aforesaid, I do order and declare that all
persons held as slaves within said designated
States and parts of States are, and hencefor-
ward shall be, free ; and that the Executive
Government of the United States, including
the military and naval authorities thereof, will
recognize and maintain the freedom of said
persons.

And I hereby enjoin upon the people so declared to be free to abstain from all violence,
unless in necessary self-defence ; and I recom-
mend to them that, in all cases when allowed,
they labor faithfully for reasonable wages.

And I further declare and make known that
such persons of suitable condition will be received into the armed service of the United
States to garrison forts, positions, stations, and

other places, and to man vessels of all sorts in said service.

And upon this act, sincerely believed to be an act of justice, warranted by the Constitution upon military necessity, I invoke the considerate judgment of mankind and the gracious favor of Almighty God.

In witness whereof, I have hereunto set my hand, and caused the seal of the United States to be affixed.

[L. S.]   Done at the city of Washington, this first day of January, in the year of our Lord one thousand eight hundred and sixty-three, and of the independence of the United States of America the eighty-seventh.

ABRAHAM LINCOLN.

By the President : WILLIAM H. SEWARD, Secretary of State.

Ship of State and Pilot

May, 1863

[The following remarks were made to a committee from the Presbyterian General Assembly. It had presented Lincoln with resolutions endorsing his administration. His short acknowledging speech is eloquent of his feeling of responsibility, and of the necessity that the administration and the party should always be held subordinate to the government though factions might rise or fall.]

It has been my happiness to receive testimonies of a similar nature from, I believe, all denominations of Christians. They are all loyal, but perhaps not in the same degree or in the same numbers; but I think they all claim to be loyal. This to me is most gratifying, because from the beginning I saw that the issue of our great struggle depended on the Divine interposition and favor. If we had that, all would be well. The proportions of this rebellion were not for a long time understood. I saw that it involved the greatest difficulties, and would call forth all the powers of the whole country. The end is not yet.

The point made in your paper is well taken

Ship of State and Pilot

as to the "government" and "the administration" in whose hands are these interests. I fully appreciate its correctness and justice. In my administration I may have committed some errors. It would be indeed remarkable if I had not. I have acted according to my best judgment in every case. The views expressed by the committee accord with my own; and on this principle "the government" is to be supported though "the administration" may not in every case wisely act. As a pilot I have used my best exertions to keep afloat our Ship of State, and shall be glad to resign my trust at the appointed time to another pilot more skilful and successful than I may prove. In every case and at all hazards the government must be perpetuated. Relying, as I do, upon the Almighty Power, and encouraged as I am by these resolutions which you have just read, with the support which I receive from Christian men, I shall not hesitate to use all the means at my control to secure the termination of this rebellion and will hope for success.

I sincerely thank you for this interview, this pleasant mode of presentation, and the General Assembly for their patriotic support in these resolutions.

Speech to 166th Ohio Regiment

August 22, 1864

Soldiers: I suppose you are going home to
see your families and friends. For the services
you have done in this great struggle in which
we are all engaged, I present you sincere thanks
for myself and the country.

I almost always feel inclined, when I happen
to say anything to soldiers, to impress upon
them, in a few brief remarks, the importance
of success in this contest. It is not merely for
to-day, but for all time to come, that we should
perpetuate for our children's children that great
and free government which we have enjoyed
all our lives. I beg you to remember this, not
merely for my sake, but for yours. I happen
temporarily, to occupy this White House I
am a living witness that any one of your children may look to come here as my father's child
has. It is in order that each one of you may
have, through this free government which we
have enjoyed, an open field and a fair chance
for your industry, enterprise, and intelligence ;
that you may all have equal privileges in the
race of life, with all its desirable human aspira-

Speech to 166th Ohio Regiment

tions. It is for this the struggle should be maintained, that we may not lose our birthright—not only for one, but for two or three years. The nation is worth fighting for, to secure such an inestimable jewel.

Response to Serenade

November 10, 1864

[This little speech was called forth by the news of Lincoln's re-election as President.]

It has long been a grave question whether any government, not too strong for the liberties of its people, can be strong enough to maintain its existence in great emergencies. On this point the present rebellion brought our republic to a severe test, and a presidential election occurring in regular course during the rebellion, added not a little to the strain.

If the loyal people united were put to the utmost of their strength by the rebellion, must they not fail when divided and partially paralyzed by a political war among themselves? But the election was a necessity. We cannot have free government without elections; and if the rebellion could force us to forego or postpone a national election, it might fairly claim to have already conquered and ruined us. The strife of the election is but human nature practically applied to the facts of the case. What has occurred in this case must ever recur in similar cases. Human nature will not change. In any future great national trial, compared

Response to Serenade

with the men of this, we shall have as weak and as strong, as silly and as wise, as bad and as good. Let us, therefore, study the incidents of this as philosophy to learn wisdom from, and none of them as wrongs to be revenged. But the election, along with its incidental and undesirable strife, has done good too. It has demonstrated that a people's government can sustain a national election in the midst of a great civil war. Until now, it has not been known to the world that this was a possibility. It shows, also, how sound and how strong we still are. It shows that, even among candidates of the same party, he who is most devoted to the Union and most opposed to treason can receive most of the people's votes. It shows, also, to the extent yet known, that we have more men now than we had when the war began. Gold is good in its place, but living, brave, patriotic men are better than gold.

But the rebellion continues, and now that the election is over, may not all having a common interest reunite in a common effort to save our common country? For my own part, I have striven and shall strive to avoid placing any obstacle in the way. So long as I have been here I have not willingly planted a thorn in any man's bosom. While I am deeply sensible to the high compliment of a re-election, and duly grateful, as I trust, to Almighty God for having directed my countrymen to a right conclusion, as I think, for their own good, it adds nothing

to my satisfaction that any other man may be
disappointed or pained by the result.

May I ask those who have not differed with
me to join with me in this same spirit toward
those who have? And now let me close by
asking three hearty cheers for our brave soldiers and seamen and their gallant and skilful
commanders.

Reply to Committee on the Electoral Count

February 9, 1865

[Lincoln had been renominated for the Presidency by the Republican Convention which met in Baltimore on June 7, 1864, and was elected on November 8 by a plurality of nearly half a million in the popular vote. In the Electoral College he had 212 votes to 21 for McClellan.]

WITH deep gratitude to my countrymen for this mark of their confidence ; with a distrust of my own ability to perform the duty required under the most favorable circumstances, and now rendered doubly difficult by existing national perils ; yet with a firm reliance on the strength of our free government, and the eventual loyalty of the people to the just principles upon which it is founded, and above all with an unshaken faith in the Supreme Ruler of nations, I accept this trust. Be pleased to signify this to the respective Houses of Congress.

The Last Address in Public

April 11, 1865

[Only three days before his assassination, Lincoln made a speech on the subject of Reconstruction—his last public address. Triumph then filled the air; two days before, Lee had surrendered at Appomattox. Yet no hint of overconfidence, much less arrogance, can be found in this speech. It is full of the broad wisdom that avoids the consideration of details until controlling principles can be established. And the extracts that follow show the tolerance, the single-mindedness for the good of the nation as a whole, that ennobled the patriot's closing days.]

We meet this evening not in sorrow, but in gladness of heart. The evacuation of Petersburg and Richmond, and the surrender of the principal insurgent army, give hope of a righteous and speedy peace, whose joyous expression cannot be restrained. In the midst of this, however, He from whom all blessings flow must not be forgotten. A call for a national thanksgiving is being prepared, and will be duly promulgated. Nor must those whose harder part gives us the cause of rejoicing be overlooked. Their honors

The Last Address in Public

must not be parceled out with others. I myself was near the front, and had the high pleasure of transmitting much of the good news to you; but no part of the honor for plan or execution is mine. To General Grant, his skilful officers and brave men, all belongs. The gallant navy stood ready, but was not in reach to take active part.

By these recent successes the reinauguration of the national authority — reconstruction — which has had a large share of thought from the first, is pressed much more closely upon our attention. It is fraught with great difficulty. Unlike a case of war between independent nations, there is no authorized organ for us to treat with — no one man has authority to give up the rebellion for any other man. We simply must begin with and mold from disorganized and discordant elements. Nor is it a small additional embarrassment that we, the loyal people, differ among ourselves as to the mode, manner, and measure of reconstruction. As a general rule, I abstain from reading the reports of attacks upon myself, wishing not to be provoked by that to which I cannot properly offer an answer. In spite of this precaution, however, it comes to my knowledge that I am much censured for some supposed agency in setting up and seeking to sustain the new tate government of Louisiana.

In this I have done just so much as, and no more than, the public knows. In the annual message of December, 1863, and in the accompanying proclamation, I presented a plan of reconstruction, as the phrase goes, which I promised, if adopted by any State, should be acceptable to and sustained by the executive government of the nation. I distinctly stated that this was not the only plan which might possibly be acceptable, and I also distinctly protested that the executive claimed no right to say when or whether members should be admitted to seats in Congress from such States. This plan was in advance submitted to the then Cabinet, and distinctly approved by every member of it. One of them suggested that I should then and in that connection apply the Emancipation Proclamation to the theretofore excepted parts of Virginia and Louisiana; that I should drop the suggestion about apprenticeship for freed people, and that I should omit the protest against my own power in regard to the admission of members to Congress. But even he approved every part and parcel of the plan which has since been employed or touched by the action of Louisiana.

．　　．　　．　　．　　．　　．

As to sustaining it, my promise is out, as before stated. But as bad promises are

The Last Address in Public

better broken than kept, I shall treat this as a bad promise, and break it whenever I shall be convinced that keeping it is adverse to the public interest; but I have not yet been so convinced. I have been shown a letter on this subject, supposed to be an able one, in which the writer expresses regret that my mind has not seemed to be definitely fixed on the question whether the seceded States, so called, are in the Union or out of it. It would perhaps add astonishment to his regret were he to learn that since I have found professed Union men endeavoring to make that question, I have purposely foreborne any public expression upon it. As appears to me, that question has not been, nor yet is, a practically material one, and that any discussion of it, while it thus remains practically immaterial, could have no effect other than the mischievous one of dividing our friends. As yet, whatever it may hereafter become, that question is bad as the basis of a controversy, and good for nothing at all — a merely pernicious abstraction.

We all agree that the seceded States, so called, are out of their proper practical relation with the Union, and that the sole object of the government, civil, and military, in regard to those States is to again get them into that proper practical relation. I believe that it is not only possible, but in fact easier,

to do this without deciding or even con‑
sidering whether these States have ever been
out of the Union, than with it. Finding
themselves safely at home, it would be
utterly immaterial whether they had ever
been abroad.

. . . .

I repeat the question: Can Louisiana be
brought into proper practical relation with
the Union sooner by sustaining or by dis‑
carding her new State government? What
has been said of Louisiana will apply gener‑
ally to other States. And yet so great
peculiarities pertain to each State, and such
important and sudden changes occur in the
same State, and withal so new and unpre‑
cedented is the whole case that no exclusive
and inflexible plan can safely be prescribed
as to details and collaterals. Such exclusive
and inflexible plan would surely become a
new entanglement. Important principles
may and must be inflexible. In the present
situation, as the phrase goes, it may be my
duty to make some new announcement to
the people of the South. I am considering,
and shall not fail to act when satisfied that
action will be proper.

Lincoln's Gettysburg Address

(Delivered at the Dedication of the National Cemetery, November 19, 1863)

Fourscore and seven years ago our fathers brought forth on this continent, a new nation, conceived in liberty, and dedicated to the proposition that all men are created equal.

Now we are engaged in a great civil war, testing whether that nation, or any nation so conceived and so dedicated, can long endure. We are met on a great battlefield of that war. We have come to dedicate a portion of that field, as a final resting-place of those who here gave their lives that that nation might live. It is altogether fitting and proper that we should do this.

But, in a larger sense, we cannot dedicate— we cannot consecrate—we cannot hallow—this ground. The brave men, living and dead, who struggled here have consecrated it, far above our poor power to add or detract. The world will little note, nor long remember what we say here, but it can never forget what they did here. It is for us the living, rather, to be dedicated here to the unfinished work which they who fought here have thus far so nobly advanced.

Abraham Lincoln

It is rather for us to be here dedicated to the great task remaining before us—that from these honored dead we take increased devotion to that cause for which they gave the last full measure of devotion—that we here highly resolve that these dead shall not have died in vain—that this nation, under God, shall have a new birth of freedom—and that government of the people, by the people, for the people, shall not perish from the earth.

Letter to McClellan

February 3, 1862

[General McClellan had succeeded General Scott on November 1, 1861, as Commander-in-Chief (under the President) of all the armies of the United States. On January 31, 1862, the President had issued his "Special War Order No. 1," directing a forward movement of the Army of the Potomac. This order conflicted with plans which McClellan had formed, and he remonstrated. Lincoln's reply is a good illustration of his power of compact statement, as well as of his mastery of the military situation.]

Executive Mansion, Washington, February 3, 1862.

MAJOR-GENERAL McCLELLAN:

MY DEAR SIR: You and I have distinct and different plans for a movement of the Army of the Potomac—yours to be down the Chesapeake, up the Rappahannock to Urbana, and across land to the terminus of the railroad on the York River; mine to move directly to a point on the railroad southwest of Manassas.

If you will give me satisfactory answers to the following questions, I shall gladly yield my plan to yours.

First. Does not your plan involve a greatly

larger expenditure of time and money than mine?

Second. Wherein is a victory more certain by your plan than mine?

Third. Wherein is a victory more valuable by your plan than mine?

Fourth. In fact, would it not be less valuable in this, that it would break no great line of the enemy's communications, while mine would?

Fifth. In case of disaster, would not a retreat be more difficult by your plan than mine?

Yours truly,

ABRAHAM LINCOLN

Maior-General McClellan.

To Seward

June 28, 1862

[This letter was written to W. H. Seward, the Secretary of State, shortly after the Union victories in Kentucky and Tennessee and upon the Mississippi River, in the spring of 1862.]

Executive Mansion, June 28, 1862.

HON. W. H. SEWARD:

MY DEAR SIR: My view of the present condition of the war is about as follows:

The evacuation of Corinth and our delay by the flood in the Chickahominy have enabled the enemy to concentrate too much force in Richmond for McClellan to successfully attack. In fact there soon will be no substantial rebel force anywhere else. But if we send all the force from here to McClellan, the enemy will, before we can know of it, send a force from Richmond and take Washington. Or if a large part of the western army be brought here to McClellan, they will let us have Richmond, and retake Tennessee, Kentucky, Missouri, etc. What should be done is to hold what we have in the West, open the Mississippi, and take Chattanooga and East Tennessee without more. A reasonable force should in every event be kept about Washington for its protection. Then let the country give us a hundred thousand new troops in the shortest possible time. which, added to McClellan directly or indirectly, will take Richmond without endangering any other place which we now hold, and will substantially end the war. I expect to maintain this contest until successful, or till I die, or am conquered, or my term expires, or Congress or the country forsake me ; and I would publicly appeal to the country for this new force were it not that I fear a general panic and stampede would follow, so hard it is to have a thing understood as it really is. I think the new force should be all, or nearly all, infantry, principally because such can be raised most cheaply and quickly.

Yours very truly,

A. Lincoln.

To Mrs. Lincoln

[Always touching was the **President's** affection, anxiety and playfulness in matters concerning his wife and his "dear Tad"— even in the most crowded days of politics and warfare.]

December 21, 1862

Washington.

MRS. A. LINCOLN, Continental Hotel:
Do not come on the night train. It is too cold. Come in the morning.

A. LINCOLN.

———

June 9, 1863

Washington.

MRS. LINCOLN, Philadelphia:
Think you had better put "Tad's" pistol away. I had an ugly dream about him.

A. LINCOLN.

———

September 21, 1863

Washington.

MRS. A. LINCOLN,
    Fifth Avenue Hotel, New York:
The air is so clear and cool and apparently healthy that I would be glad for you to come.

Nothing very particular but I would be glad
to see you and Tad.

A. LINCOLN.

April 28, 1864

Telegraphed from Executive Mansion,
Washington.

MRS. A. LINCOLN,
Metropolitan Hotel, New York.:
The draft will go to you. Tell Tad the
goats and father are very well, especially
the goats.

A. LINCOLN.

To the Workingmen of Manchester

January 19, 1863

[The blockade of Confederate ports during the war was naturally a severe blow to the English manufacturing centres like Manchester, which had depended upon the Southern States for their supply of cotton. But the working classes of England, in marked contrast with the upper classes, displayed strong Union sympathies throughout the struggle. An address from the Manchester workingmen called forth this admirable reply from the President.]

Executive Mansion, Washington, January 19, 1863.

To the Workingmen of Manchester : I have the honor to acknowledge the receipt of the address and resolutions which you sent me on the eve of the new year. When I came, on the 4th of March, 1861, through a free and constitutional election to preside in the Government of the United States, the country was found at the verge of civil war. Whatever might have been the cause, or whosesoever the fault, one duty, paramount to all others, was before me, namely, to maintain and preserve at once the Constitution and the integrity of the Federal Republic. A conscientious purpose to perform this duty is the key to all the measures of administration which have been and to all which will hereafter be pursued. Under our frame of government and my official oath, I could not depart from this purpose if I would. It is not always in the power of governments to enlarge or restrict the scope of moral results which follow the policies that they may deem it necessary for the public safety from time to time to adopt.

I have understood well that the duty of self-preservation rests solely with the American people; but I have at the same time been aware that favor or disfavor of foreign nations might have a material influence in enlarging or prolonging the struggle with disloyal men in which the country is engaged. A fair examination of history has served to authorize a belief that the past actions and influences of the United States were generally regarded as having been beneficial toward mankind. I have, therefore, reckoned upon the forbearance of nations. Circumstances—to some of which you kindly allude—induce me especially to expect that if justice and good faith should be practised by the United States, they would encounter no hostile influence on the part of Great Britain. It is now a pleasant duty to acknowledge the demonstration you have given of your desire that a spirit of amity and peace toward this country may prevail in the councils of your Queen, who is respected and esteemed in your own country only more than she is by the kindred nation which has its home on this side of the Atlantic.

I know and deeply deplore the sufferings which the workingmen at Manchester, and in

To Workingmen of Manchester

all Europe, are called to endure in this crisis.
It has been often and studiously represented
that the attempt to overthrow this government,
which was built upon the foundation of human
rights, and to substitute for it one which should
rest exclusively on the basis of human slavery,
was likely to obtain the favor of Europe.
Through the action of our disloyal citizens, the
workingmen of Europe have been subjected to
severe trials, for the purpose of forcing their
sanction to that attempt. Under the circum
stances, I cannot but regard your decisive utter
ances upon the question as an instance of
sublime Christian heroism which has not been
surpassed in any age or in any country. It is
indeed an energetic and reinspiring assurance
of the inherent power of truth, and of the ultimate and universal triumph of justice, human
ity, and freedom. I do not doubt that the sen
timents you have expressed will be sustained
by your great nation ; and, on the other hand
I have no hesitation in assuring you that they
will excite admiration, esteem, and the most re
ciprocal feelings of friendship among the Ameri
can people. I hail this interchange of senti
ment, therefore, as an augury that whatever
else may happen, whatever misfortune may be-
tail your country or my own, the peace and
friendship which now exist between the two
nations will be, as it shall be my desire to make
them, perpetual.

Abraham Lincoln.

To Burnside

July 27, 1863

[This telegram is noticeable for its brief but comprehensive description of General Grant.]

War Department, Washington, July 27, 1863.

MAJOR-GENERAL BURNSIDE, Cincinnati, Ohio:

Let me explain. In General Grant's first despatch after the fall of Vicksburg, he said, among other things, he would send the Ninth Corps to you. Thinking it would be pleasant to you, I asked the Secretary of War to telegraph you the news. For some reasons never mentioned to us by General Grant, they have not been sent, though we have seen outside intimations that they took part in the expedition against Jackson. General Grant is a copious worker and fighter, but a very meager writer or telegrapher. No doubt he changed his purpose in regard to the Ninth Corps for some sufficient reason, but has forgotten to notify us of it.

A. LINCOLN.

To Astor, Roosevelt and Sands

November 9, 1863

Executive Mansion, Washington, D. C.
Messrs. J. J. Astor, Jr., R. B. Roosevelt,
and Nathaniel Sands:

Gentlemen: Upon the subject of your letter, I have to say that it is beyond my province to interfere with New York City politics; that I am very grateful to General Dix for the zealous and able military and quasi-civil support he has given the government during the war, and that if the people of New York should tender him the mayoralty and he accept it, nothing on that subject could be more satisfactory to me. In this I must not be understood as saying aught against any one, or as attempting the least degree of dictation in the matter.

To state it in another way, if General Dix's present relation to the General Government lays any restraint upon him in this matter. I wish to remove that restraint.

Yours truly,

A. LINCOLN.

To Edward Everett

November 20, 1863

[See the note prefixed to Lincoln's Gettys burg address.]

Executive Mansion, Washington, November 20, 1863.
HON. EDWARD EVERETT:

MY DEAR SIR : Your kind note of to-day is received. In our respective parts yesterday, you could not have been excused to make a short address, nor I a long one. I am pleased to know that, in your judgment, the little I did say was not entirely a failure. Of course I knew Mr. Everett would not fail, and yet, while the whole discourse was eminently satisfactory, and will be of great value, there were passages in it which transcended my expectations. The point made against the theory of the General Government being only an agency whose principals are the States, was new to me, and, as I think, is one of the best arguments for the national supremacy. The tribute to our noble women for their angel ministering to the suffering soldiers surpasses in its way, as do the subjects of it, whatever has gone before.

Our sick boy, for whom you kindly inquire, we hope is past the worst.

Your obedient servant.

A. LINCOLN

Tc Grant

April 30, 1864

[The sprir g campaign of 1864 marked "the beginning of the end" of the Rebellion. This letter is one of many proofs of Lincoln's absolute confidei ce in Grant's generalship.]

Executiv Mansion, Washington, April 30, 1864

LIEUTENANT GENERAL GRANT:

Not expecting to see you again before the spring campaign opens, I wish to express in this way my entire satisfaction with what you have done up to this time, so far as I understand it. The particulars of your plans I neither know nor seek to know. You are vigilant and self-reliant; and, pleased with this, I wish not to obtrude any constraints or restraints upon you. While I am very anxious that any great disaster or capture of our men in great numbers shall be avoided, I know these points are less likely to escape your attention than they would be mine. If there is anything wanting which is within my power to give, do not fail to let me know it. And now, with a brave army and a just cause, may God sustain you.

Yours very truly,

A. LINCOLN.

To William Cullen Bryant

June 27, 1864

[No lack of courtesy can be discerned in this reply to the venerable Bryant, poet, author, and even at the time of that writing, with a thirty-six-year record as editor-in-chief of the New York *Evening Post*. Yet Lincoln's firm words in conclusion could have left no doubt that, in all directions wherein his own information shone clear, his course was not to be altered by newspaper criticisms from any source whatever.]

Executive Mansion, Washington.

HON. WILLIAM CULLEN BRYANT:

MY DEAR SIR: Yours of the twenty-fifth has just been handed me by the Secretary of the Navy. The tone of the letter, rather than any direct statement in it, impresses me as a complaint that Mr. Henderson should have been removed from office, and arrested; coupled with the single suggestion that he be restored if he shall establish his innocence.

I know absolutely nothing of the case except as follows: Monday last, Mr. Welles came to me with the letter of dismissal already written, saying he thought proper to show it to me before sending it. I asked him the charges, which he stated in a general

To William Cullen Bryant

way. With as much emphasis as I could, I said: "Are you entirely certain of his guilt?" He answered that he was, to which I replied: "Then send the letter."

Whether Mr. Henderson was a supporter of my second nomination I neither knew nor inquired, nor even thought of. I shall be very glad indeed if he shall, as you anticipate, establish his innocence; or, to state it more strongly and properly, "if the government shall fail to establish his guilt." I believe, however, the man who made the affidavit was of as spotless reputation as Mr. Henderson, until he was arrested on what his friends insist was outrageously insufficient evidence. I know the entire city government of Washington, with many other respectable citizens, appealed to me in his behalf as a greatly injured gentleman.

While the subject is up, may I ask whether the *Evening Post* has not assailed me for supposed too lenient dealing with persons charged with fraud and crime? And that in cases of which the *Post* could know but little of the facts? I shall certainly deal as leniently with Mr. Henderson as I have felt it my duty to deal with others, notwithstanding any newspaper assaults.

> Your obedient servant,
> A. LINCOLN.

To Thurlow Weed

March 15, 1865

[This most interesting letter, written a month before Lincoln's assassination, should be read in connection with the second inaugural address.]

Executive Mansion, Washington, March 15, 1865.

DEAR MR. WEED:

Every one likes a compliment. Thank you for yours on my little notification speech and on the recent inaugural address. I expect the latter to wear as well as—perhaps better than—anything I have produced; but I believe it is not immediately popular. Men are not flattered by being shown that there has been a difference of purpose between the Almighty and them. To deny it, however, in this case, is to deny that there is a God governing the world. It is a truth which I thought needed to be told, and, as whatever of humiliation there is in it falls most directly on myself, I thought others might afford for me to tell it.

Truly yours,

A. LINCOLN.

CHARLES LAMB

THE
POCKET UNIVERSITY
VOLUME V   PART II

LAMB

EDITED BY
BLISS PERRY

PUBLISHED FOR
NELSON DOUBLEDAY, INC.
BY
DOUBLEDAY, PAGE & COMPANY
GARDEN CITY   NEW YORK
1924

*Acknowledgment is due to A. C. Armstrong & Son for permission
to use selections from the text of their edition of Lamb's
letters, edited by Alfred Ainger*

CONTENTS

Editor's Introduction

THE only editorial discomfort in selecting a couple of hundred of Lamb's choicest pages has arisen from a sense of the excellence of those other pages that have not been taken. Even were the choice to be made from the "Essays of Elia" alone, the chooser must needs stand like a boy under an apple-tree, with pockets stuffed already, and yet eyeing and comparing and half tempted to trade his plunderings for some of the fruit still hanging on the tree,—so hazardous is this business of making sure that one has the best. To justify in set terms one's instinctive preference among the delicate-flavoured fruitage of Lamb's genius is a still more difficult task, and perhaps not altogether worth doing, even were it possible.

In casting about for some word or other of preface, however, it occurred to the editor to consult the latest literary handbook and discover how Lamb was faring nowadays at the hands of the professional critics. He found first some five pages of Biography,—all about the Temple and Christ's Hospital, the South Sea House, the India House, the home life,

Editor's Introduction

tragic and gay, the publication of essays and verses, the long holiday at last and the quiet ending; then three closely-printed pages of Bibliography on Lamb's style; and finally, the following ten Particular Characteristics, each vouched for by various competent critics and proved by illustrative examples: 1. Quaintness—Fondness for the Antique. 2. Tenderness —Sympathy with Humanity. 3. Graceful Ease —Companionability. 4. Amiable Humour. 5. Wit—Epigram—Paronomasia. (This last, O unclassical reader, means that Lamb liked to make puns;—and they were the worst, that is to say, the best, in the world!) 6. Self-Reflection—Unselfish Egoism. 7. Delicate Fancy. 8. Melancholy. 9. Critical Acumen. 10. Discursiveness.

To all who love Particular Characteristics the foregoing list is warmly commended. It has been borrowed without leave and is reproduced here with a kind of awe. For in the two editions of Lamb which the editor knows best there are marginal comments in great plenty, and yet nothing whatever is said about Particular Characteristics. One edition is a tattered paper-bound affair, with boyish pencil marks drawn long and black along the margin of many a delicious paragraph. The other, still more highly prized, is annotated throughout in the minute beautiful handwriting of that lover of Lamb's memory and fit companion for Lamb himself, the late Professor Dodd of

Editor's Introduction

Williams College. But even in those luminous and scholarly footnotes there is nothing about Graceful Ease or Amiable Humour or Critical Acumen. Professor Dodd was somewhat old-fashioned in his tastes, and never had the advantage of Laboratory Courses in literature.

To confess the truth, this little volume is equally innocent of any disciplinary intention. It is not designed to train the critical faculties of anybody. It is meant to be slipped into the pocket and pulled out when one feels like reading Lamb. The nine "Essays of Elia" which it contains are among the most delightful of that rare company and are fairly representative of the range of Lamb's moods and tastes. Some of them, like "Dream-Children" and "The Superannuated Man," are frankly autobiographical, and all of them, it is needless to say, have a good deal of Lamb in them. To one reading him for the first time they will prove, it is hoped, a happy introduction, and they contain many of those passages which old friends of one of the friendliest of writers find themselves reading over and over with a perpetually renewed and deepened pleasure.

A distinctive feature of the book is the inclusion of a dozen or more of Lamb's letters, which have not hitherto been put within easy reach of the general public. These letters not only, as Mr. Birrell has remarked, "do the reader good by stealth," but explain many facts and motives of Lamb's life that would otherwise be misinterpreted. It has been thought best to print here even those two most personal letters to Coleridge concerning the great tragedy of the Lamb household, because without a knowledge of Lamb's domestic circumstances the sweetness and heroism of his nature cannot be fully perceived. The letters to his friends Manning, Wordsworth, Bernard Barton and others, reflect the surroundings of Lamb's later life and make more complete the expression of a lovable personality.

Lamb's poetry is now little read, but some of it is so graceful and felicitous that a volume of selections from his writings should certainly include a few specimens of his verse. I have chosen the "Farewell to Tobacco" (it was not a very long farewell, by the way!) the daintily lyrical lines entitled "She is Going," and "The Old Familiar Faces," whose simple, haunting pathos has given it a secure immortality among English minor poetry.

BLISS PERRY.

Essays

ESSAYS

THE TWO RACES OF MEN

THE human species, according to the best theory I can form of it, is composed of two distinct races, *the men who borrow, and the men who lend.* To these two original diversities may be reduced all those impertinent classifications of Gothic and Celtic tribes, white men, black men, red men. All the dwellers upon earth, "Parthians, and Medes, and Elamites," flock hither, and do naturally fall in with one or other of these primary distinctions. The infinite superiority of the former, which I choose to designate as the *great race,* is discernible in their figure, port, and a certain instinctive sovereignty. The latter are born degraded. "He shall serve his brethren." There is something in the air of one of this cast, lean and suspicious; contrasting with the open, trusting, generous manners of the other.

Observe who have been the greatest borrowers of all ages Alcibiades—Falstaff—Sir Rich

3

ard Steele—our late incomparable Brinsley,—
what a family likeness in all four!

What a careless, even deportment hath your
borrower! what rosy gills! what a beautiful reliance on Providence doth he manifest,—taking
no more thought than lilies! What contempt
for money,—accounting it (yours and mine especially) no better than dross! What a liberal
confounding of those pedantic distinctions of
meum and *tuum!* or rather, what a noble sim-
plification of language, (beyond Tooke,) re-
solving these supposed opposites into one clear,
intelligible pronoun adjective! What near approaches doth he make to the primitive *community,*—to the extent of one-half of the principle at least.

He is the true taxer who "calleth all the
world up to be taxed;" and the distance is as
vast between him and *one of us,* as subsisted
between the Augustan Majesty and the poorest
obolary Jew that paid his tribute-pittance at
Jerusalem!—His exactions, too, have such a
cheerful, voluntary air!—so far removed from
your sour parochial or state-gatherers,—those
ink-horn varlets, who carry their want of welcome in their faces! He cometh to you with a
smile, and troubleth you with no receipt; confining himself to no set season. Every day is
his Candlemas, or his Feast of Holy Michael.
He applieth the *lene tormentum* of a pleasant
look to your purse,—which to that gentle
warmth expands her silken leaves, as naturally

as the cloak of the traveller, for which sun and wind contended. He is the true Propontic which never ebbeth,—the sea which taketh handsomely at each man's hand. In vain the victim, whom he delighteth to honour, struggles with destiny; he is in the net. Lend therefore cheerfully, O man ordained to lend, that thou lose not in the end, with thy worldly penny, the reversion promised. Combine not preposterously in thine own person the penalties of Lazarus and of Dives;—but when thou seest the proper authority coming, meet it smilingly, as it were half-way. Come, a handsome sacrifice! See how light *he* makes of it! Strain not courtesies with a noble enemy.

Reflections like the foregoing were forced upon my mind by the death of my old friend, Ralph Bigod, Esq., who parted this life on Wednesday evening; dying, as he had lived, without much trouble. He boasted himself a descendant from mighty ancestors of that name, who heretofore held ducal dignities in this realm. In his actions and sentiments he belied not the stock to which he pretended. Early in life he found himself invested with ample revenues; which, with that noble disinterestedness which I have noticed as inherent in men of the *great race,* he took almost immediate measures entirely to dissipate and bring to nothing: for there is something revolting in the idea of a king holding a private purse; and the thoughts of Bigod were all regal. Thus

furnished by the very act of disfurnishment,
—getting rid of the cumbersome luggage of
riches, more apt (as one sings)

To slacken virtue, and abate her edge,
Than prompt her to do aught may merit praise,

he set forth, like some Alexander, upon his
great enterprise, "borrowing and to borrow!"

In his periegesis, or triumphant progress
throughout this island, it has been calculated
that he laid a tythe part of the inhabitants under contribution. I reject this estimate as
greatly exaggerated; but having had the honour of accompanying my friend divers times
in his perambulations about this vast city, I
own I was greatly struck at first with the prodigious number of faces we met who claimed
a sort of respectful acquaintance with us. He
was one day so obliging as to explain the
phenomenon. It seems these were his tribu-
taries; feeders of his exchequer; gentlemen,
his good friends, (as he was pleased to express
himself,) to whom he had occasionally been be-
holden for a loan. Their multitudes did no
way disconcert him. He rather took a pride in
numbering them; and, with Comus, seemed
pleased to be "stocked with so fair a herd."

With such sources, it was a wonder he con-
trived to keep his treasury always empty. He
did it by force of an aphorism, which he had
often in his mouth, that "money kept longer
than three days stinks." So he made use of it

Essays

while it was fresh. A good part he drank
away (for he was an excellent tosspot); some
he gave away, the rest he threw away, literally
tossing and hurling it violently from him—as
boys do burrs, or as if it had been infectious—
into ponds, or ditches, or deep holes, inscrutable cavities of the earth;—or he would bury
it (where he would never seek it again) by a
river's side under some bank, which (he would
facetiously observe) paid no interest; but out
away from him it must go peremptorily, as
Hagar's offspring into the wilderness, while it
was sweet. He never missed it. The streams
were perennial which fed his fisc. When new
supplies became necessary, the first person that
had the felicity to fall in with him, friend or
stranger, was sure to contribute to the de-
ficiency; for Bigod had an *undeniable* way with
him. He had a cheerful, open exterior, a quick
jovial eye, a bald forehead, just touched with
grey (*cana fides*). He anticipated no excuse,
and found none. And, waiving for a while my
theory as to the *great race,* I would put it to
the most untheorising reader, who may at times
have disposable coin in his pocket, whether it is
not more repugnant to the kindliness of his
nature to refuse such a one as I am describing,
than to say *no* to a poor petitionary rogue
(your bastard borrower) who, by his mumping
visnomy, tells you that he expects nothing better; and, therefore, whose preconceived notions

and expectations you do in reality so much less shock in the refusal.

When I think of this man,—his fiery glow of heart, his swell of feeling,—how magnificent, how *ideal* he was; how great at the midnight hour; and when I compare with him the companions with whom I have associated since, I grudge the saving of a few idle ducats, and think that I am fallen into the society of *lenders* and *little* men.

To one like Elia whose treasures are rather cased in leather covers than closed in iron coffers, there is a class of alienators more formidable than that which I have touched upon; I mean your *borrowers of books*—those mutilators of collections, spoilers of the symmetry of shelves, and creators of odd volumes. There is Comberbatch, matchless in his depredations!

That foul gap in the bottom shelf facing you, like a great eye-tooth knocked out—(you are now with me in my little back study in Bloomsbury, reader)—with the huge Switzer-like tomes on each side (like the Guildhall giants, in their reformed posture, guardant of nothing) once held the tallest of my folios, *Opera Bonaventuræ,* choice and massive divinity, to which its two supporters (school divinity also, but of a lesser calibre,—Bellarmine, and Holy Thomas) showed but as dwarfs,—itself an Ascapart!—*that* Comberbatch abstracted upon the faith of a theory he holds, which is more easy, I confess, for me to suffer by than to refute, namely, that "the title to property in a book, (my Bonaventure, for instance,) is in exact ratio to the claimant's powers of under-standing and appreciating the same." Should he go on acting upon this theory, which of our shelves is safe?

The slight vacuum in the left-hand case—two shelves from the ceiling—scarcely distin-guishable but by the quick eye of a loser—was whilom the commodious resting-place of Brown on Urn Burial. C. will hardly allege that he knows more about that treatise than I do, who introduced it to him, and was indeed the first (of the moderns) to discover its beau-ties; but so have I known a foolish lover to praise his mistress in the presence of a rival more qualified to carry her off than himself. Just below, Dodsley's dramas want their fourth volume, where Vittoria Corombona is! The remainder nine are as distasteful as Priam's refuse sons when the Fates *borrowed* Hector. Here stood the *Anatomy* of *Melancholy,* in sober state. There loitered the *Complete Ang-ler;* quiet as in life, by some stream side. In yonder nook, John Buncle, a widower-volume, with "eyes closed," mourns his ravished mate.

One justice I must do my friend, that if he sometimes, like the sea, sweeps away a treas-ure, at another time, sea-like, he throws up as rich an equivalent to match it. I have a small under-collection of this nature, (my friend's gatherings in his various calls,) picked up, he

has forgotten at what odd places, and deposited
with as little memory at mine. I take in these
orphans, the twice-deserted. These proselytes
of the gate are welcome as the true Hebrews.
There they stand in conjunction; natives and
naturalized. The latter seem as little disposed
to inquire out their true lineage as I am.—I
charge no warehouse-room for these deodands,
nor shall ever put myself to the ungentlemanly
trouble of advertising a sale of them to pay
expenses.

To lose a volume to C. carries some sense
and meaning in it. You are sure that he will
make one hearty meal on your viands, if he can
give no account of the platter after it. But
what moved thee, wayward, spiteful K—, to be
so importunate to carry off with thee, in spite
of tears and adjurations to thee to forbear, the
Letters of that princely woman, the thrice noble
Margaret Newcastle?—knowing at the time,
and knowing that I knew also, thou most as-
suredly wouldst never turn over one leaf of the
illustrious folio:—what but the mere spirit of
contradiction, and childish love of getting the
better of thy friend?—Then (worst cut of all!)
to transport it with thee to the Gallican land—

Unworthy land to harbour such a sweetness,
A virtue in which all ennobling thoughts dwelt,
Pure thoughts, kind thoughts, high thoughts,
   her sex's wonder!

hadst thou not thy play-books, and books of
tests and fancies, about thee, to keep thee

merry, even as thou keepest all companies with
thy quips and mirthful tales? Child of the
Green-room, it was unkindly done of thee.
Thy wife, too, that part-French, better-part
English woman!—that *she* could fix upon no
other treatise to bear away, in kindly token of
remembering us, than the works of Folke•
Greville, Lord Brooke,—of which no French-
man, nor woman of France, Italy, or England,
was ever by nature constituted to comprehend
a title!—*Was there not Zimmerman on Solitude?*

Reader, if haply thou art blest with a moderate collection, be shy of showing it; or if thy
heart overfloweth to lend them, lend thy books;
but let it be to such a one as S. T. C.: he will
return them (generally anticipating the time
appointed) with usury, enriched with annota-
tions tripling their value. I have had experience. Many are these precious MSS. of his—
(in *matter* oftentimes, and almost in *quantity*
not unfrequently, vying with the originals) in
no very clerkly hand—legible in my Daniel; in
old Burton, in Sir Thomas Browne; and those
abstruser cogitations of the Greville,—now,
alas, wandering in Pagan lands! I counsel
thee, shut not thy heart nor thy library against
S. T. C.

NEW YEAR'S EVE

Every man hath two birthdays: two days, at
least, in every year, which set him upon revolv-

ing the lapse of time, as it affects his mortal duration. The one is that which in an especial manner he termeth *his*. In the gradual desuetude of old observances, this custom of solemnizing our proper birthday hath nearly passed away, or is left to children, who reflect nothing at all about the matter, nor understand anything in it beyond cake and orange. But the birth of a New Year is of an interest too wide to be pretermitted by king or cobbler. No one ever regarded the first of January with indifference. It is that from which all date their time, and count upon what is left. It is the nativity of our common Adam.

Of all sound of all bells—(bells, the music nighest bordering upon heaven)—most solemn and touching is the peal which rings out the Old Year. I never hear it without a gathering-up of my mind to a concentration of all the images that have been diffused over the past twelvemonth; all I have done or suffered, performed or neglected, in that regretted time. I begin to know its worth, as when a person dies. It takes a personal colour; nor was it a poetical flight in a contemporary when he exclaimed—

I saw the skirts of the departing Year.

It is no more than what in sober sadness every one of us seems to be conscious of, in that awful leave taking. I am sure I felt it, and all felt it with me, last night; though some of my companions affected rather to manifest

Essays

an exhilaration at the birth of the coming year, than any very tender regrets for the decease of its predecessor. But I am none of those who—

Welcome the coming, speed the parting guest.

I am naturally, beforehand, shy of novelties, —new books, new faces, new years,—from some mental twist which makes it difficult in me to face the prospective. I have almost ceased to hope; and am sanguine only in the prospects of other (former) years. I plunge into foregone visions and conclusions. I encounter pell-mell with past disappointments. I am armour-proof against old discouragements. I forgive, or overcome in fancy, old adversaries. I play over again *for love,* as the gamesters phrase it, games for which I once paid so dear. I would scarce now have any of those untoward accidents and events of my life reversed. I would no more alter them than the incidents of some well-contrived novel. Methinks it is better that I should have pined away seven of my goldenest years, when I was thrall to the fair hair and fairer eyes of Alice W—n, than that so passionate a love-adventure should be lost. It was better that our family should have missed that legacy, which old Dorrell cheated us of, than that I should have at this moment two thousand pounds *in banco,* and be without the idea of that specious old rogue.

13

Charles Lamb

In a degree beneath manhood, it is my infirmity to look back upon those early days. Do I advance a paradox, when I say, that, skipping over the intervention of forty years, a man may have leave to love *himself,* without the imputation of self-love?

If I know aught of myself, no one whose mind is introspective—and mine is painfully so —can have a less respect for his present identity than I have for the man Elia. I know him to be light, and vain, and humoursome; a notorious***; addicted to****: averse from counsel, neither taking it nor offering it;—*** besides; a stammering buffoon; what you will; lay it on, and spare not: I subscribe to it all, and much more than thou canst be willing to lay at his door: but for the child Elia, that "other me," there, in the back-ground, I must take leave to cherish the remembrance of that young master,—with as little reference, I protest, to this stupid changeling of five-and-forty as if it had been a child of some other house, and not of my parents. I can cry over its patient small-pox at five, and rougher medicaments. I can lay its poor fevered head upon the sick pillow at Christ's, and wake with it in surprise at the gentle posture of maternal tenderness hanging over it, that unknown had watched its sleep. I know how it shrank from any the least colour of falsehood. God help thee, Elia, how art thou changed!—Thou art sophisticated.—I know how honest, how cour-

geous (for a weakling) it was,—how religious, how imaginative, how hopeful! From
what have I not fallen, if the child I remember
was indeed myself, and not some dissembling
guardian, presenting a false identity, to give
the rule to my unpractised steps, and regulate
the tone of my moral being!

That I am fond of indulging beyond a hope
of sympathy, in such retrospection, may be the
symptom of some sickly idiosyncrasy. Or is it
owing to another cause: simply, that being
without wife or family, I have not learned to
project myself enough out of myself; and having no offspring of my own to dally with, I
turn back upon memory, and adopt my own
early idea as my heir and favourite? If these
speculations seem fantastical to thee, reader, (a
busy man perchance,) if I tread out of the way
of thy sympathy, and am singularly conceited
only, I retire, impenetrable to ridicule, under
the phantom cloud of Elia.

The elders, with whom I was brought up,
were of a character not likely to let slip the
sacred observance of any old institution; and
the ringing out of the Old Year was kept by
them with circumstances of peculiar ceremony.
In those days the sound of those midnight
chimes, though it seemed to raise hilarity in all
around me, never failed to bring a train of
pensive imagery into my fancy. Yet I then
scarce conceived what it meant, or thought of
it as a reckoning that concerned me. Not child-

hood alone, but the young man till thirty, never feels practically that he is mortal. He knows it indeed, and, if need were he could preach a homily on the fragility of life; but he brings it not home to himself, any more than in a hot June we can appropriate to our imagination the freezing days of December. But now (shall I confess a truth?) I feel these audits but too powerfully. I begin to count the probabilities of my duration, and to grudge at the expenditure of moments and shortest periods, like misers' farthings. In proportion as the years both lessen and shorten, I set more count upon their periods, and would fain lay my ineffectual finger upon the spoke of the great wheel. I am not content to pass away "like a weaver's shuttle." Those metaphors solace me not, nor sweeten the unpalatable draught of mortality. I care not to be carried with the tide that smoothly bears human life to eternity; and reluct at the inevitable course of destiny. I am in love with this green earth,—the face of town and country,—the unspeakable rural solitudes, and the sweet security of streets. I would set up my tabernacle here I am content to stand still at the age to which I am arrived,—I and my friends,—to be no younger, no richer, no handsomer. I do not want to be weaned by age; or drop, like mellow fruit, as they say, into the grave. Any alteration, on this earth of mine, in diet or in lodging, puzzles and discomposes me. My household gods plant a terrible

fixed foot, and are not rooted up without blood.
They do not willingly seek Lavinian shores.
A new state of being staggers me.

Sun, and sky, and breeze, and solitary walks,
and Summer holidays, and the greenness of
fields, and the delicious juices of meats and
fishes, and society, and the cheerful glass, and
candle-light, and fireside conversations, and innocent vanities, and jests, and *irony itself,—*
do these things go out with life?

Can a ghost laugh, or shake his gaunt sides,
when you are pleasant with him?

And you, my midnight darlings, my Folios!
must I part with the intense delight of having
you (huge armfuls) in my embraces? Must
knowledge come to me, if it come at all, by
some awkward experiment of intuition, and no
longer by this familiar process of reading?

Shall I enjoy friendships there, wanting the
smiling indications which point me to them
here,—the recognisable face,—the "sweet assurance of a look?"

In Winter this intolerable disinclination to
dying—to give it its mildest name—does more
especially haunt and beset me. In a genial
August noon, beneath a sweltering sky, death
is almost problematic. At those times do such
poor snakes as myself enjoy an immortality.
Then we expand and burgeon. Then we are
as strong again, as valiant again, as wise again,
and a great deal taller. The blast that nips
and shrinks me, puts me in thoughts of death.

Charles Lamb

All things allied to the insubstantial wait upon that master feeling,—cold, numbness, dreams, perplexity, moonlight itself, with its shadowy and spectral appearances,—that cold ghost of the sun, or Phœbus's sickly sister, like that innutritious one denounced in the Canticles:—I am none of her minions; I hold with the Persian.

Whatsoever thwarts, or puts me out of my way, brings death into my mind. All partial evils, like humours, run into that capital plague-sore. I have heard some profess an indifference to life. Such hail the end of their existence as a port of refuge; and speak of the grave as of some soft arms, in which they may slumber as on a pillow. Some have wooed Death; but out upon thee, I say, thou foul, ugly phantom! I detest, abhor, execrate, and (with Friar John) give thee to six score thousand devils, as in no instance to be excused or tolerated, but shunned as an universal viper,—to be branded, proscribed, and spoken evil of! In no way can I be brought to digest thee, thou thin, melancholy *Privation*, or more frightful and confounding *Positive*!

Those antidotes, prescribed against the fear of thee, are altogether frigid and insulting, like thyself. For what satisfaction hath a man, that he shall "lie down with kings and emperors in death," who in his lifetime never greatly coveted the society of such bedfellows?—or, forsooth, that "so shall the fairest face appear?"—

why, to comfort me, must Alice W——n be a goblin? More than all, I conceive disgust at those impertinent and misbecoming familiarities inscribed upon your ordinary tombstones Every deadman must take upon himself to be lecturing me with his odious truism, that "Such as he now is I must shortly be." Not so shortly, friend, perhaps, as thou imaginest. In the meantime I am alive. I move about. I am worth twenty of thee. Know thy betters! Thy New Years' days are past. I survive, a jolly candidate for 1821. Another cup of wine!—and while that turncoat bell, that just now mournfully chanted the obsequies of 1820 departed, with changed notes lustily rings in a successor, let us attune to its peal the song made on a like occasion, by hearty, cheerful Mr. Cotton :—

THE NEW YEAR

Hark! the cock crows! and yon bright star
Tells us, the day himself's not far.
And see where, breaking from the night,
He gilds the western hills with light!
With him old Janus doth appear,
Peeping into the future year,
With such a look as seems to say
The prospect is not good that way.
Thus do we rise ill sights to see,
And 'gainst ourselves do prophesy;
When the prophetic fear of things
A more tormenting mischief brings,
More full of soul-tormenting gall
Than direst mischiefs can befall.

Charles Lamb

But stay! but stay! methinks my sight
Better inform'd by clearer light,
Discerns sereneness in that brow,
That all contracted seem'd but now.
His revers'd face may show distaste,
And frown upon the ills are past;
But that which this way looks is clear,
And smiles upon the New-born Year.
He looks too from a place so high,
The year lies open to his eye;
And all the moments open are
To the exact discoverer.
Yet more and more he smiles upon
The happy revolution.
Why should we then suspect or fear
The influences of a year,
So smiles upon us the first morn,
And speaks us good so soon as born?
Plague on't! the last was ill enough,
This cannot but make better proof;
Or, at the worst, as we brush'd through
The last, why so we may this too;
And then the next in reason shou'd
Be superexcellently good:
For the worst ills (we daily see)
Have no more perpetuity
Than the best fortunes that do fall;
Which also bring us wherewithal
Longer their being to support,
Than those do of the other sort:
And who has one good year in three,
And yet repines at destiny,
Appears ungrateful in the case,
And merits not the good he has.
Then let us welcome the New Guest
With lusty brimmers of the best;
Mirth always should Good Fortune meet,
And renders e'en Disaster sweet:
And though the Princess turn her back,
Let us but line ourselves with sack,

We better shall by far hold out,
Till the next Year she face about.

How say you, reader—do not these verses
smack of the rough magnanimity of the old
English vein? Do they not fortify like a cordial; enlarging the heart, and productive of
sweet blood, and generous spirits, in the con-
coction? Where be those puling fears of
death, just now expressed or affected?—
Passed like a cloud—absorbed in the purging
sunlight of clear poetry—clean washed away
by a wave of genuine Helicon, your only Spa
for these hypochondries. And now another
cup of the generous! and a merry New Year,
and many of them to you all, my masters!

IMPERFECT SYMPATHIES

I am of a constitution so general, that it con-
sorts and sympathizeth with all things. I have
no antipathy, or rather idiosyncrasy in any
thing. Those natural repugnancies do not
touch me; nor do I behold with prejudice the
French, Italian, Spaniard, or Dutch.—*Religio
Medici.*

THAT the author of the Religio Medici,
mounted upon the airy stilts of abstraction,
conversant about notional and conjectural es-
sences, in whose categories of Being the possible took the upper hand of the actual, should
have overlooked the impertinent individualities

21

of such poor concretions as mankind, is not **much to be admired. It is rather to be wondered at, that in the genus of animals he should have condescended to distinguish that species at all.** For myself,—earthbound and fettered to the scene of my activities,—

Standing on earth, not rapt above the sky,

I confess that I do feel the differences of mankind, national or individual, to an unhealthy excess. I can look with no indifferent eye upon things or persons. Whatever is, is to me a matter of taste or distaste; or when once it becomes indifferent, it begins to be disrelishing. I am, in plainer words, a bundle of prejudices —made up of likings and dislikings—the veriest thrall to sympathies, apathies, antipathies. In a certain sense, I hope it may be said of me that I am a lover of my species. I can feel for all indifferently, but I cannot feel towards all equally. The more purely English word that expresses sympathy, will better explain my meaning. I can be a friend to a worthy man, who upon another account cannot be my mate or *fellow*. I cannot *like* all people alike.[1]

---

[1] I would be understood as confining myself to the subject of *imperfect sympathies*. To nations or classes of men there can be no direct antipathy. There may be individuals born and constellated so opposite to another individual nature, that the same sphere cannot hold them. I have met with my moral antipodes, and can

Essays

I have been trying all my life to like Scotchmen, and am obliged to desist from the experiment in despair. They cannot like me; and in truth, I never knew one of that nation who attempted to do it. There is something more plain and ingenuous in their mode of proceeding. We know one another at first sight. There is an order of imperfect intellects (under which mine must be content to rank) which in its constitution is essentially anti-Caledonian. The owners of the sort of faculties I allude to

believe the story of two persons meeting (who never saw one another before in their lives) and instantly fighting.

————We by proof find there should be
'Twixt man and man such an antipathy,
That though he can show no just reason why
For any former wrong or injury,
Can neither find a blemish in his fame,
Nor aught in face or feature justly blame,
Can challenge or accuse him of no evil,
Yet notwithstanding hates him as a devil.

The lines are from old Heywood's "Hierarchie of Angels," and he subjoins a curious story in confirmation, of a Spaniard who attempted to assassinate a King Ferdinand of Spain, and being put to the rack could give no other reason for the deed but an inveterate antipathy which he had taken to the first sight of the King.

————The cause which to that act compell'd
    him
Was, he ne'er loved him since he first beheld
    him.

have minds rather suggestive than comprehensive. They have no pretences to much clearness or precision in their ideas, or in their manner of expressing them. Their intellectual wardrobe (to confess fairly) has few whole pieces in it. They are content with fragments and scattered pieces of Truth. She presents no full front to them—a feature or side-face at the most. Hints and glimpses, germs and crude essays at a system, is the utmost they pretend to. They beat up a little game peradventure, and leave it to knottier heads, more robust constitutions, to run it down. The light that lights them is not steady and polar, but mutable and shifting: waxing, and again waning. Their conversation is accordingly. They will throw out a random word in or out of season, and be content to let it pass for what it is worth. They cannot speak always as if they were upon their oath, but must be understood, speaking or writing, with some abatement. They seldom wait to mature a proposition, but e'en bring it to market in the green ear. They delight to impart their defective discoveries as they arise, without waiting for their full development. They are no systematizers, and would but err more by attempting it. Their minds, as I said before, are suggestive merely. The brain of a true Caledonian (if I am not mistaken) is constituted upon quite a different plan. His Minerva is born in panoply. You are never admitted to see his ideas in their growth—if indeed they do grow, and are not rather put together upon principles of clock-work. You never catch his mind in an undress. He never hints or suggests anything, but unlades his stock of ideas in perfect order and completeness. He brings his total wealth into company, and gravely unpacks it. His riches are always about him. He never stoops to catch a glittering something in your presence to share it with you, before he quite knows whether it be true touch or not. You cannot cry *halves* to anything that he finds. He does not find, but bring. You never witness his first apprehension of a thing. His understanding is always at its meridian: you never see the first dawn, the early streaks. He has no falterings of self-suspicion. Surmises, guesses, misgivings, half-intuitions, semi-consciousness, partial illuminations, dim instincts, embryo conceptions, have no place in his brain or vocabulary. The twilight of dubiety never falls upon him. Is he orthodox—he has no doubts. Is he an infidel—he has none either. Between the affirmative and the negative there is no border-land with him. You cannot hover with him upon the confines of truth, or wander in the maze of a probable argument. He always keeps the path. You cannot make excursions with him, for he sets you right. His taste never fluctuates. His morality never abates. He cannot compromise, or understand middle actions. There can be but a right and a wrong. His conversation is as a book. His affirmations have the sanctity of an oath. You must speak upon the square with him. He stops a metaphor like a suspected person in an enemy's country. "A healthy book!"—said one of his countrymen to me, who had ventured to give that appellation to John Buncle,—"Did I catch rightly what you said? I have heard of a man in health, and of a healthy state of body, but I do not see how that epithet can be properly applied to a book." Above all, you must beware of indirect expressions before a Caledonian. Clap an extinguisher upon your irony if you are unhappily blest with a vein of it. Remember you are upon your oath. I have a print of a graceful female after Leonardo da Vinci, which I was showing off to Mr. * * *. After he had examined it minutely, I ventured to ask him how he liked MY BEAUTY, (a foolish name it goes by among my friends,) when he very gravely assured me that "he had considerable respect for my character and talents," (so he was pleased to say,) "but had not given himself much thought about the degree of my personal pretensions." The misconception staggered me, but did not seem much to disconcert him. Persons of this nation are particularly fond of affirming a truth, which nobody doubts. They do not so properly affirm as annunciate it. They do indeed appear to have such a love of truth (as if, like virtue, it were valuable for

Essays

itself) that all truth becomes equally valuable, whether the proposition that contains it be new or old, disputed, or such as is impossible to become a subject of disputation. I was present not long since at a party of North Britons, where a son of Burns was expected, and happened to drop a silly expression (in my South British way,) that I wished it were the father instead of the son—when four of them started up at once to inform me that "that was impossible, because ne was dead." An impracticable wish, it seems, was more than they could conceive. Swift has hit off this part of their character, namely their love of truth, in his biting way, but with an illiberality that necessarily confines the passage to the margin.[1] The tediousness of these people is certainly provoking. I wonder if they ever tire one another!—In my early life I had a passionate fondness for the poetry of Burns. I have sometimes foolishly hoped to ingratiate myself with

---

[1]There are some people who think they sufficiently acquit themselves, and entertain their company, with relating facts of no consequence, not at all out of the road of such common incidents as happen every day; and this I have observed more frequently among the Scots than any other nation, who are very careful not to omit the minutest circumstances of time or place: which kind of discourse, if it were not a little relieved by the uncouth terms and phrases, as well as accent and gesture, peculiar to that country, would be hardly tolerable.— *Hints towards an Essay on Conversation.*

27

his countrymen by expressing it. But I have always found that a true Scot resents your admiration of his compatriot, even more than he would your contempt of him. The latter he imputes to your "imperfect acquaintance with many of the words which he uses;" and the same objection makes it a presumption in you to suppose that you can admire him. Thomson they seem to have forgotten. Smollett they have neither forgotten nor forgiven, for his delineation of Rory and his companion, upon their first introduction to our metropolis. Speak of Smollett as a great genius, and they will retort upon you Hume's History compared with *his* Continuation of it. What if the historian had continued Humphrey Clinker?

I have, in the abstract, no disrespect for Jews. They are a piece of stubborn antiquity, compared with which Stonehenge is in its nonage. They date beyond the pyramids. But I should not care to be in habits of familiar intercourse with any of that nation. I confess that I have not the nerves to enter their synagogues. Old prejudices cling about me. I cannot shake off the story of Hugh of Lincoln. Centuries of injury, contempt, and hate, on the one side,—of cloaked revenge, dissimulation, and hate, on the other, between our and their fathers, must and ought to affect the blood of the children. I cannot believe it can run clear and kindly yet; or that a few fine words, such as candour, liberality, the light of a nineteenth century, can

close up the breaches of so deadly a disunion.
A Hebrew is nowhere congenial to me. He is
least distasteful on 'Change, for the mercantile spirit levels all distinctions, as all are beau-
ties in the dark. I boldly confess that I do not
relish the approximation of Jew and Christian, which has become so fashionable. The re-
ciprocal endearments have, to me, something
hypocritical and unnatural in them. I do not
like to see the Church and Synagogue kissing
and congeeing in awkward postures of an affected civility. If *they* are converted, why do
they not come over to us altogether? Why
keep up a form of separation, when the life of
it is fled? If they can sit with us at table, why
do they keck at our cookery? I do not understand these half convertites. Jews christian-
izing—Christians judaizing—puzzle me. I like
fish or flesh. A moderate Jew is a more confounding piece of anomaly than a wet Quaker.
The spirit of the synagogue is essentially *sepa-
rative*. B——— would have been more in
keeping if he had abided by the faith of his
forefathers. There is a fine scorn in his face,
which nature meant to be of Christians. The
Hebrew spirit is strong in him, in spite of his
proselytism. He cannot conquer the Shibboleth.
How it breaks out, when he sings, "The Children of Israel passed through the Red Sea!"
The auditors, for the moment, are as Egyp-
tians to him, and he rides over our necks in
triumph. There is no mistaking him. B———

has a strong expression of sense in his countenance, and it is confirmed by his singing. The
foundation of his vocal excellence is sense. He
sings with understanding, as Kemble delivered
dialogue. He would sing the Commandments,
and give an appropriate character to each prohibition. His nation, in general, have not over-
sensible countenances. How should they?—but
you seldom see a silly expression among them.
Gain, and the pursuit of gain, sharpen a man's
visage. I never heard of an idiot being born
among them. Some admire the Jewish female
physiognomy. I admire it, but with trembling.
Jael had those full, dark, inscrutable eyes.

In the Negro countenance you will often
meet with strong traits of benignity. I have felt
yearnings of tenderness towards some of these
faces—or rather masks—that have looked out
kindly upon one in casual encounters in the
streets and highways. I love what Fuller
beautifully calls these—"images of God cut in
ebony." But I should not like to associate with
them, to share my meals and my good-nights
with them—because they are black.

I love Quaker ways and Quaker worship. I
venerate the Quaker principles. It does me
good for the rest of the day when I meet any
of their people in my path. When I am ruffled
or disturbed by any occurrence, the sight or
quiet voice of a Quaker acts upon me as a
ventilator, lightening the air, and taking off a
load from the bosom. But I cannot like the

Essays

Quakers (as Desdemona would say) "to live with them." I am all over sophisticated—with humours, fancies, craving hourly sympathy. I must have books, pictures, theatres, chit-chat, scandal, jokes, ambiguities, and a thousand whim-whams, which their simpler taste can do without. I should starve at their primitive banquet. My appetites are too high for the salads which (according to Evelyn) Eve dressed for the angel, my gusto too excited

To sit a guest with Daniel at his pulse.

The indirect answers which Quakers are often found to return to a question put to them may be explained, I think, without the vulgar assumption that they are more given to evasion and equivocating than other people. They naturally look to their words more carefully, and are more cautious of committing themselves. They have a peculiar character to keep up on this head. They stand in a manner upon their veracity. A Quaker is by law exempted from taking an oath. The custom of resorting to an oath in extreme cases, sanctified as it is by all religious antiquity, is apt (it must be confessed) to introduce into the laxer sort of minds the notion of two kinds of truth—the one applicable to the solemn affairs of justice, and the other to the common proceedings of daily intercourse. As truth bound upon the conscience by an oath can be but truth, so in the common affirmations of the shop and the market-place a latitude is expected and conceded upon questions wanting this solemn covenant. Some thing less than truth satisfies. It is common to hear a person say, "You do not expect me to speak as if I were upon my oath." Hence a great deal of incorrectness and inadvertency, short of falsehood, creeps into ordinary conversation; and a kind of secondary or laic-truth is tolerated, where clergy-truth—oath-truth, by the nature of the circumstances, is not required. A Quaker knows none of this distinction. His simple affirmation being received, upon the most sacred occasions, without any further test, stamps a value upon the words which he is to use upon the most indifferent topics of life. He looks to them, naturally, with more severity. You can have of him no more than his word. He knows, if he is caught tripping in a casual expression, he forfeits, for himself, at least, his claim to the invidious exemption. He knows that his syllables are weighed; and how far a consciousness of this particular watchfulness, exerted against a person, has a tendency to produce indirect answers, and a diverting of the question by honest means, might be illustrated, and the practice justified, by a more sacred example than is proper to be adduced upon this occasion. The admirable presence of mind, which is notorious in Quakers upon all contingencies, might be traced to this imposed self-watchfulness—if it did not seem rather an humble and secular

scion of that old stock of religious constancy,
which never bent or faltered, in the Primitive
Friends, or gave way to the winds of persecu-
tion, to the violence of judge or accuser, under
trials and racking examinations. "You will
never be the wiser if I sit here answering your
questions till midnight," said one of those upright Justicers to Penn, who had been putting
law-cases with a puzzling subtlety. "Thereafter
as the answers may be," retorted the Quaker.
The astonishing composure of this people is
sometimes ludicrously displayed in lighter instances. I was travelling in a stage-coach with
three male Quakers, buttoned up in the strait-
est non-conformity of their sect. We stopped
to bait at Andover, where a meal, partly tea
apparatus, partly supper, was set before us. My
friends confined themselves to the tea-table. I
in my way took supper. When the landlady
brought in the bill, the eldest of my companions
discovered that she had charged for both meals.
This was resisted. Mine hostess was very clam-
ourous and positive. Some mild arguments were
used on the part of the Quakers, for which the
heated mind of the good lady seemed by no
means a fit recipient. The guard came in with
his usual peremptory notice. The Quakers
pulled out their money and formally tendered
it—so much for tea. I, in humble imitation,
tendering mine for the supper which I had
taken. She would not relax in her demand.
So they all three quietly put up their silver, as

did myself, and marched out of the room, the eldest and gravest going first, with myself closing up the rear, who thought I could not do better than follow the example of such grave and warrantable personages. We got in. The steps went up. The coach drove off. The murmurs of mine hostess, not very indistinctly or ambiguously pronounced, became after a time inaudible; and now my conscience, which the whimsical scene had for a while suspended, beginning to give some twitches, I waited, in the hope that some justification would be offered by these serious persons for the seeming injustice of their conduct. To my great surprise not a syllable was dropped on the subject. They sat as mute as at a meeting. At length the eldest of them broke silence, by inquiring of his next neighbour, "Hast thee heard how indigos go at the India House?" and the question operated as a soporific on my moral feeling as far as Exeter.

DREAM CHILDREN; A REVERIE

CHILDREN love to listen to stories about their elders, when *they* were children; to stretch their imagination to the conception of a traditionary great-uncle or grandame whom they never saw. It was in this spirit that my little ones crept about me the other evening to hear about their great-grandmother Field, who lived in a great house in Norfolk, (a hundred times

bigger than that in which they and papa lived,)
which had been the scene (so at least it was
generally believed in that part of the country)
of the tragic incidents which they had lately
become familiar with from the ballad of the
Children in the Wood. Certain it is that the
whole story of the children and their uncle was
to be seen fairly carved out in wood upon the
chimney-piece of the great hall, the whole story
down to the Robin Redbreasts; till a foolish
rich person pulled it down to set up a marble
one of modern invention in its stead, with no
story upon it. Here Alice put out one of her
dear mother's looks, too tender to be called up-
braiding. Then I went on to say how religious
and how good their great-grandmother Field
was, how beloved and respected by everybody,
though she was not indeed the mistress of this
great house, but had only the charge of it
(and yet in some respects she might be said to
be the mistress of it too) committed to her by
the owner, who preferred living in a newer and
more fashionable mansion which he had purchased somewhere in the adjoining county; but
still she lived in it in a manner as if it had been
her own, and kept up the dignity of the great
house in a sort while she lived, which afterwards came to decay, and was nearly pulled
down, and all its old ornaments stripped and
carried away to the owner's other house, where
they were set up, and looked as awkward as if
some one were to carry away the old tombs

they had seen lately at the Abbey, and stick
them up in Lady C.'s tawdry gilt drawing-
room. Here John smiled, as much as to say,
"that would be foolish indeed." And then I
told how, when she came to die, her funeral
was attended by a concourse of all the poor,
and some of the gentry too, of the neighbour-
hood for many miles round, to show their respect for her memory, because she had been
such a good and religious woman; so good indeed that she knew all the Psaltery by heart,
ay, and a great part of the Testament besides.
Here little Alice spread her hands. Then I told
what a tall, upright, graceful person their
great-grandmother Field once was; and how in
her youth she was esteemed the best dancer,
(here Alice's little right foot played an involuntary movement, till, upon my looking grave,
it desisted,) the best dancer, I was saying, in
the county, till a cruel disease, called a cancer,
came, and bowed her down with pain; but it
could never bend her good spirits, or make
them stoop, but they were still upright, because she was so good and religious. Then I
told how she was used to sleep by herself in a
lone chamber of the great lone house; and how
she believed that an apparition of two infants
was to be seen at midnight gliding up and down
the great staircase near where she slept, but
she said "those innocents would do her no
harm;" and how frightened I used to be,
though in those days I had my maid to sleep

with me, because I was never half so good or
religious as she; and yet I never saw the infants. Here John expanded all his eyebrows
and tried to look courageous. Then I told how
good she was to all her grandchildren, having
us to the great house in the holidays, where I
in particular used to spend many hours by myself, in gazing upon the old busts of the twelve
Cæsars, that had been Emperors of Rome, till
the old marble heads would seem to live again,
or I to be turned into marble with them; how
I never could be tired with roaming about that
huge mansion, with its vast empty rooms, with
their worn-out hangings, fluttering tapestry,
and carved oaken panels, with the gilding almost rubbed out; sometimes in the spacious
old-fashioned gardens, which I had almost to
myself, unless when now and then a solitary
gardening man would cross me; and how the
nectarines and peaches hung upon the walls,
without my ever offering to pluck them, because they were forbidden fruit, unless now
and then; and because I had more pleasure in
strolling about among the old melancholy-look-
ing yew-trees, or the firs, and picking up the
red berries, and the fir-apples, which were good
for nothing but to look at—or in lying about
upon the fresh grass with all the fine garden
smells around me—or basking in the orangery,
till I could almost fancy myself ripening too
along with the oranges and the limes in that
grateful warmth—or in watching the dace that

darted to and fro in the fish-pond at the bottom
of the garden, with here and there a great sulky
pike hanging midway down the water in
silent state, as if it mocked at their
impertinent friskings,—I had more pleasure in these busy-idle diversions than in
all the sweet flavours of peaches, nectarines, oranges, and such-like common
baits for children. Here John slyly deposited
back upon the plate a bunch of grapes, which,
not unobserved by Alice, he had meditated dividing with her, and both seemed willing to re-
linquish them for the present as irrelevant.
Then, in somewhat a more heightened tone, I
told how, though their great-grandmother Field
loved all her grandchildren, yet in an especial
manner she might be said to love their uncle,
John L——, because he was so handsome and
spirited a youth, and a king to the rest of us;
and, instead of moping about in solitary cor-
ners, like some of us, he would mount the most
mettlesome horse he could get, when but an
imp no bigger than themselves, and make it
carry him half over the county in a morning,
and join the hunters when there were any out;
(and yet he loved the old great house and gardens too, but had too much spirit to be always
pent up within their boundaries;) and how
their uncle grew up to man's estate as brave as
he was handsome, to the admiration of everybody, but of their great-grandmother Field
most especially; and how he used to carry me

upon his back when I was a lame-footed boy,
(for he was a good bit older than I,) many a
mile when I could not walk for pain; and how
in after life he became lame-footed too, and
I did not always, I fear, make allowances
enough for him when he was impatient, and in
pain, nor remember sufficiently how considerate
he had been to me when I was lame-footed;
and how when he died, though he had not been
dead an hour, it seemed as if he had died a
great while ago, such a distance there is betwixt life and death; and how I bore his death
as I thought pretty well at first, but afterwards
it haunted and haunted me; and though I did
not cry or take it to heart as some do, and as
I think he would have done if I had died, yet
I missed him all day long, and knew not till
then how much I had loved him. I missed his
kindness, and I missed his crossness, and
wished him to be alive again, to be quarrelling
with him, (for we quarrelled sometimes,) rather
than not have him again, and was as uneasy
without him as he their poor uncle, must have
been when the doctor took off his limb.—Here
the children fell a crying, and asked if their
little mourning which they had on was not for
Uncle John and they looked up, and prayed me
not to go on about their uncle, but to tell them
some stories about their pretty dead mother.
Then I told how for seven long years, in hope
sometimes, sometimes in despair, yet persisting
ever, I courted the fair Alice W——n; and,

as much as children could understand, I explained to them what coyness, and difficulty,
and denial, meant in maidens—when suddenly,
turning to Alice, the soul of the first Alice
looked out at her eyes with such a reality of
re-presentment, that I became in doubt which
of them stood there before me, or whose that
bright hair was; and while I stood gazing, both
the children gradually grew fainter to my view,
receding, and still receding, till nothing at last
but two mournful features were seen in the
uttermost distance, which, without speech,
strangely impressed upon me the effects of
speech: "We are not of Alice, nor of thee, nor
are we children at all. The children of Alice
call Bartrum father. We are nothing; less
than nothing, and dreams. We are only what
might have been, and must wait upon the tedious shores of Lethe millions of ages before we
have existence and a name"——and immediately awaking, I found myself quietly seated in
my bachelor arm-chair, where I had fallen
asleep, with the faithful Bridget unchanged by
my side; but John L. (or James Elia) was gone
forever.

A DISSERTATION UPON ROAST PIG

MANKIND, says a Chinese manuscript, which
my friend M—— was obliging enough to
read and explain to me, for the first seventy
thousand ages ate their meat raw, clawing or

biting it from the living animal, just as they do in Abyssinia to this day. This period is not obscurely hinted at by their great Confucius in the second chapter of his Mundane Mutations, where he designates a kind of golden age by the term Cho-fang, literally the Cooks' Holiday. The manuscript goes on to say, that the art of roasting, or rather broiling (which I take to be the elder brother) was accidentally discovered in the manner following. The swine-herd Ho-ti, having gone out into the woods one morning, as his manner was, to collect mast for his hogs, left his cottage in the care of his eldest son, Bo-bo, a great lubberly boy, who being fond of playing with fire, as younkers of his age commonly are, let some sparks escape into a bundle of straw, which kindling quickly, spread the conflagration over every part of their poor mansion, till it was reduced to ashes. Together with the cottage, (a sorry antediluvian make-shift of a building, you may think it,) what was of much more importance, a fine litter of new-farrowed pigs, no less than nine in number, perished. China pigs have been esteemed a luxury all over the East, from the remotest periods that we read of. Bo-bo was in the utmost consternation, as you may think, not so much for the sake of the tenement, which his father and he could easily build up again with a few dry branches, and the labour of an hour or two at any time, as for the loss of the pigs. While he was thinking what he should say to his father, and wringing his hands over the smoking remnants of one of those untimely sufferers, an odour assailed his nostrils, unlike any scent which he had before experienced. What could it proceed from? Not from the burnt cottage: he had smelt that smell before: indeed this was by no means the first accident of the kind which had occurred through the negligence of this unlucky young fire-brand. Much less did it resemble that of any known herb, weed, or flower. A premonitory moistening at the same time overflowed his nether lip. He knew not what to think. He next stooped down to feel the pig, if there were any signs of life in it. He burnt his fingers, and to cool them he applied them in his booby fashion to his mouth. Some of the crumbs of the scorched skin had come away with his fingers, and for the first time in his life, (in the world's life indeed, for before him no man had known it,) he tasted *crackling!* Again he felt and fumbled at the pig. It did not burn him so much now, still he licked his fingers from a sort of habit. The truth at length broke into his slow understanding, that it was the pig that smelt so, and the pig that tasted so delicious; and surrendering himself up to the new-born pleasure, he fell to tearing up whole handfulls of the scorched skin with the flesh next it, and was cramming it down his throat in his beastly fashion, when his sire entered amid the smoking rafters, armed with retributory cudgel, and finding how affairs stood, began to rain blows upon the young rogue's shoulders as thick as hail-stones, which Bo-bo heeded not any more than if they had been flies. The tickling pleasure which he experienced in his lower regions had rendered him quite callous to any inconveniences he might feel in those remote quarters. His father might lay on, but he could not beat him from his pig, till he had fairly made an end of it, when, becoming a little more sensible of his situation, something like the following dialogue ensued :—

"You graceless whelp, what have you got there devouring? Is it not enough that you have burnt me down three houses with your dog's tricks, and be hanged to you! but you must be eating fire, and I know not what. What have you got there, I say?"

"O father, the pig, the pig! do come and taste how nice the burnt pig eats."

The ears of Ho-ti tingled with horror. He cursed his son, and he cursed himself that ever he should beget a son that should eat burnt pig.

Bo-bo, whose scent was wonderfully sharpened since morning, soon raked out another pig, and fairly rending it asunder, thrust the lesser half by main force into the fists of Ho-ti, still shouting out, "Eat, eat, eat the burnt pig, father, only taste—O Lord!"—with such-like barbarous ejaculations, cramming all the while as if he would choke.

Charles Lamb

Ho-ti trembled every joint while he grasped the abominable thing, wavering whether he should not put his son to death for an unnatural young monster, when the crackling scorching his fingers, as it had done his son's, and applying the same remedy to them, he in his turn tasted some of its flavour, which, make what sour mouths he would for a pretence, proved not altogether displeasing to him. In conclusion, (for the manuscript here is a little tedious,) both father and son fairly sat down to the mess, and never left off till they had despatched all that remained of the litter.

Bo-bo was strictly enjoined not to let the secret escape, for the neighbours would certainly have stoned them for a couple of abominable wretches, who could think of improving upon the good meat which God had sent them. Nevertheless, strange stories got about. It was observed that Ho-ti's cottage was burnt down now more frequently than ever. Nothing but fires from this time forward. Some would break out in broad day, others in the nighttime. As often as the sow farrowed, so sure was the house of Ho-ti to be in a blaze; and Ho-ti himself, which was the more remarkable, instead of chastising his son, seemed to grow more indulgent to him than ever. At length they were watched, the terrible mystery discovered, and father and son summoned to take their trial at Pekin, then an inconsiderable assize town. Evidence was given, the obnoxious

food itself produced in court, and verdict about
to be pronounced, when the foreman of the jury
begged that some of the burnt pig, of which the
culprits stood accused, might be handed into
the box. He handled it, and they all handled
it; and burning their fingers, as Bo-bo and his
father had done before them, and nature
prompting to each of them the same remedy,
against the face of all the facts, and the clearest
charge which judge had ever given,—to the
surprise of the whole court, townsfolk,
strangers, reporters, and all present—without
leaving the box, or any manner of consultation
whatever, they brought in a simultaneous verdict of Not Guilty.

The judge, who was a shrewd fellow, winked
at the manifest iniquity of the decision: and
when the court was dismissed, went privily and
bought up all the pigs that could be had for
love or money. In a few days his lordship's
town-house was observed to be on fire. The
thing took wing, and now there was nothing to
be seen but fire in every direction. Fuel and
pigs grew enormously dear all over the district.
The insurance-offices, one and all, shut up
shop. People built slighter and slighter every
day, until it was feared that the very science of
architecture would in no long time be lost to
the world. Thus this custom of firing houses
continued, till in process of time, says my
manuscript, a sage arose, like our Locke, who
made a discovery that the flesh of swine, or in-

deed of any other animal, might be cooked (*burnt,* as they called it,) without the necessity of consuming a whole house to dress it. Then first began the rude form of a gridiron. Roasting by the string or spit came in a century or two later, I forget in whose dynasty. By such slow degrees, concludes the manuscript, do the most useful and seemingly the most obvious, arts make their way among mankind.

Without placing too implicit faith in the account above given, it must be agreed that if a worthy pretext for so dangerous an experiment as setting houses on fire (especially in these days) could be assigned in favour of any culinary object, that pretext and excuse might be found in ROAST PIG.

Of all the delicacies in the whole *mundus edibilis,* I will maintain it to be the most delicate —*princeps obsoniorum.*

I speak not of your grown porkers—things between pig and pork, those hobbydehoys—but a young and tender suckling, under a moon old, guiltless as yet of the sty, with no original speck of the *amor immunditiæ,* the hereditary failing of the first parent. yet manifest—his voice as yet not broken, but something between a childish treble and a grumble—the mild forerunner or *præludium* of a grunt.

He must be roasted. I am not ignorant that our ancestors ate them seethed, or boiled; but what a sacrifice of the exterior tegument!

There is no flavour comparable, I will contend, to that of the crisp, tawny, well-watched, not over-roasted, *crackling,* as it is well called. The very teeth are invited to their share of the pleasure at this banquet in overcoming the coy, brittle resistance—with the adhesive oleaginous —O call it not fat! but an indefinable sweetness growing up to it—the tender blossoming of fat—fat cropped in the bud—taken in the shoot—in the first innocence—the cream and quintessence of the child-pig's yet pure food— the lean, no lean, but a kind of animal manna— or, rather, fat and lean (if it must be so) so blended and running into each other, that both together make but one ambrosian result, or common substance.

Behold him, while he is "doing"—it seemeth rather a refreshing warmth than a scorching heat that he is so passive to. How equably he twirleth round the string!—Now he is just done. To see the extreme sensibility of that tender age! he hath wept out his pretty eyes— radiant jellies—shooting stars.—

See him in the dish, his second cradle, how meek he lieth!—Wouldst thou have had this innocent grow up to the grossness and indocility which too often accompany maturer swinehood? Ten to one he would have proved a glutton, a sloven, an obstinate, disagreeable animal, wallowing in all manner of filthy conversation. From these sins he is happily snatched away.

Ere sin could blight or sorrow fade,
Death came with timely care.

His memory is odouriferous. No clown curseth,
while his stomach half rejecteth, the rank bacon; no coal-heaver bolteth him in reeking sau-
sages; he hath a fair sepulchre in the grateful
stomach of the judicious epicure, and for such
a tomb might be content to die.

He is the best of sapors. Pine-apple is great.
She is indeed almost too transcendent,—a delight, if not sinful, yet so like to sinning that
really a tender-conscienced person would do
well to pause,—too ravishing for mortal taste,
she woundeth and excoriateth the lips that approach her. Like lovers' kisses, she biteth: she
is a pleasure bordering on pain from the fierce-
ness and insanity of her relish; but she stoppeth
at the palate; she meddleth not with the appetite; and the coarsest hunger might barter her
consistently for a mutton-chop.

Pig (let me speak his praise) is no less pro-
vocative of the appetite than he is satisfactory
to the criticalness of the censorious palate. The
strong man may batten on him, and the weakling refuseth not his mild juices.

Unlike to mankind's mixed characters, a
bundle of virtues and vices, inexplicably inter-
twisted, and not to be unravelled without
hazard, he is good throughout. No part of him
is better or worse than another. He helpeth, as
far as his little means extend, all around. He

is the least envious of banquets. He is all
neighbours' fare.

I am one of those who freely and ungrudg-
ingly impart a share of the good things of this
life which fall to their lot (few as mine are in
this kind) to a friend, I protest I take as great
an interest in my friend's pleasures, his rel-
ishes, and proper satisfactions, as in mine own.
" Presents," I often say, " endear Absents."
Hares, pheasants, partridges, snipes, barn-door
chickens, (those " tame villatic fowl,") capons,
plovers, brawn, barrels of oysters, I dispense as
freely as I receive them. I love to taste them,
as it were, upon the tongue of my friend. But
a stop must be put somewhere. One would not,
like Lear, " give everything." I make my stand
upon pig. Methinks it is an ingratitude to the
giver of all good flavours to extra-domiciliate,
or send out of the house slightingly (under pretext of friendship, or I know not what,) a
blessing so particularly adapted, predestined, I
may say, to my individual palate.—It argues an
insensibility.

I remember a touch of conscience in this kind
at school. My good old aunt, who never parted from me at the end of a holiday without
stuffing a sweetmeat, or some nice thing into
my pocket, had dismissed me one evening with
a smoking plum-cake, fresh from the oven. In
my way to school (it was over London Bridge)
a grey-headed old beggar saluted me. (I have
no doubt, at this time of day, that he was a

counterfeit.) I had no pence to console him with, and in the vanity of self-denial, and the very coxcombry of charity, schoolboy-like, I made him a present of the whole cake. I walked on a little, buoyed up, as one is on such occasions, with a sweet soothing of self-satisfaction; but before I had got to the end of the bridge my better feelings returned, and I burst into tears, thinking how ungrateful I had been to my good aunt, to go and give her good gift away to a stranger that I had never seen before, and who might be a bad man for aught I knew; and then I thought of the pleasure my aunt would be taking in thinking that I (I myself, and not another) would eat her nice cake. And what should I say to her the next time I saw her?—how naughty I was to part with her pretty present!—and the odour of that spicy cake came back upon my recollection, and the pleasure and the curiosity I had taken in seeing her make it, and her joy when she sent it to the oven, and how disappointed she would feel that I had never had a bit of it in my mouth at last. And I blamed my impertinent spirit of almsgiving, and out-of-place hypocrisy of goodness; and above all, I wished never to see the face again of that insidious, good-for-nothing, old grey impostor.

Our ancestors were nice in their method of sacrificing these tender victims. We read of pigs whipt to death with something of a shock, as we hear of any other obsolete custom. The age of discipline is gone by, or it would be curious to inquire (in a philosophical light merely) what effect this process might have towards intenerating and dulcifying a substance naturally so mild and dulcet as the flesh of young pigs. It looks like refining a violet. Yet we should be cautious, while we condemn the inhumanity how we censure the wisdom of the practice. It might impart a gusto.

I remember an hypothesis, argued upon by the young students when I was at St. Omer's, and maintained with much learning and pleasantry on both sides, " Whether, supposing that the flavour of a pig who obtained his death by whipping (*per flagellationem extremam*) superadded a pleasure upon the palate of a man more intense than any possible suffering we can conceive in the animal, is man justified in using that method of putting the animal to death ? " I forget the decision.

His sauce should be considered : decidedly, a few bread crumbs, done up with his liver and brains, and a dash of mild sage. But banish, dear Mrs. Cook, I beseech you, the whole onion tribe. Barbecue your whole hogs to your palate, steep them in shalots, stuff them out with plantations of the rank and guilty garlic ; you cannot poison them, or make them stronger than they are ; but consider, he is a weakling—a flower.

Charles Lamb

ON SOME OF THE OLD ACTORS

THE casual sight of an old Play Bill, which I picked up the other day—I know not by what chance it was preserved so long—tempts me to call to mind a few of the Players who make the principal figure in it. It presents the cast of parts in the *Twelfth Night*, at the old Drury Lane Theatre two-and-thirty years ago. There is something very touching in these old remembrances. They make us think how we *once* used to read a Play Bill—not, as now peradventure, singling out a favourite performer, and casting a negligent eye over the rest; but spelling out every name, down to the very mutes and servants of the scene; when it was a matter of no small moment to us whether Whitfield, or Packer, took the part of Fabian; when Benson, and Burton, and Phillimore—names of small account—had an importance beyond what we can be content to attribute now to the time's best actors. " Orsino, by Mr. Barrymore." What a full Shakespearian sound it carries ! how fresh to memory arise the image and the manner of the gentle actor !

Those who have only seen Mrs. Jordan within the last ten or fifteen years can have no adequate notion of her performance of such parts as Ophelia ; Helena, in *All's Well that Ends Well ;* and Viola in this play. Her voice had latterly acquired a coarseness, which suited

well enough with her Nells and Hoydens, but
in those days it sank, with her steady, melting
eye, into the heart. Her joyous parts, in which
her memory now chiefly lives, in her youth
were outdone by her plaintive ones. There is
no giving an account how she delivered the dis-
guised story of her love for Orsino. It was no
set speech, that she had foreseen, so as to
weave it into an harmonious period, line necessarily following line, to make up the music—
yet I have heard it so spoken, or rather *read,*
not without its grace and beauty—but, when
she had declared her sister's history to be a
"blank," and that she "never told her love,"
there was a pause, as if the story had ended—
and then the image of the "worm in the bud,"
came up as a new suggestion—and the heightened image of "Patience" still followed after
that, as by some growing (and not mechanical)
process, thought springing up after thought, I
would almost say, as they were watered by her
tears. So in those fine lines—

Right loyal cantos of contemned love—
Hollow your name to the reverberate hills—

there was no preparation made in the foregoing
image for that which was to follow. She used
no rhetoric in her passion; or it was Nature's
own rhetoric, most legitimate then, when it
seemed altogether without rule or law.

Mrs. Powel (now Mrs. Renard), then in the
pride of her beauty, made an admirable Olivia.

She was particularly excellent in her unbending scenes in conversation with the Clown. I have seen some Olivias—and those very sensible actresses too—who in these interlocutions have seemed to set their wits at the jester, and to vie conceits with him in downright emulation. But she used him for her sport, like what he was, to trifle a leisure sentence or two with, and then to be dismissed, and she to be the Great Lady still. She touched the imperious fantastic humour of the character with nicety. Her fine spacious person filled the scene.

The part of Malvolio has, in my judgment, been so often misunderstood, and the *general merits* of the actor, who then played it, so unduly appreciated, that I shall hope for pardon if I am a little prolix upon these points.

Of all the actors who flourished in my time—a melancholy phrase if taken aright, reader—Bensley had most of the swell of soul, was greatest in the delivery of heroic conceptions, the emotions consequent upon the presentment of a great idea to the fancy. He had the true poetical enthusiasm—the rarest faculty among players. None that I remember possessed even a portion of that fine madness which he threw out in Hotspur's famous rant about glory, or the transports of the Venetian incendiary at the vision of the fired city. His voice had the dissonance, and at times the inspiriting effect, of the trumpet. His gait was uncouth and stiff,

but no way embarrassed by affectation; and the
thorough-bred gentleman was uppermost in
every movement. He seized the moment of
passion with greatest truth; like a faithful
clock, never striking before the time; never anticipating or leading you to anticipate. He was
totally destitute of trick and artifice. He seemed
come upon the stage to do the poet's message
simply, and he did it with as genuine fidelity as
the nuncios in Homer deliver the errands of the
gods. He let the passion or the sentiment do
its own work without prop or bolstering. He
would have scorned to mountebank it; and betrayed none of that *cleverness* which is the bane
of serious acting. For this reason, his Iago was
the only endurable one which I remember to
have seen. No spectator, from his action, could
divine more of his artifice than Othello was
supposed to do. His confessions in soliloquy
alone put you in possession of the mystery.
There were no by-intimations to make the audience fancy their own discernment so much
greater than that of the Moor—who commonly
stands like a great helpless mark, set up for
mine Ancient, and a quantity of barren spectators, to shoot their bolts at. The Iago of Bensley did not go to work so grossly. There was
a triumphant tone about the character, natural
to a general consciousness of power; but none
of that petty vanity which chuckles and cannot
contain itself upon any little successful stroke
of its knavery—as is common with your small

villains, and green probationers in mischief. It did not clap or crow before its time. It was not a man setting his wits at a child, and winking all the while at other children, who are mightily pleased at being let into the secret; but a consummate villain entrapping a noble nature into toils, against which no discernment was available, where the manner was as fathomless as the purpose seemed dark, and without motive. The part of Malvolio, in the *Twelfth Night,* was performed by Bensley with a richness and a dignity of which (to judge from some recent castings of that character) the very tradition must be worn out from the stage. No manager in those days would have dreamed of giving it to Mr. Baddeley or Mr. Parsons; when Bensley was occasionally absent from the theatre, John Kemble thought it no derogation to succeed to the part. Malvolio is not essentially ludicrous. He becomes comic but by accident. He is cold, austere, repelling; but dignified, consistent, and, for what appears, rather of an over-stretched morality. Maria describes him as a sort of Puritan; and he might have worn his gold chain with honour in one of our old round-head families, in the service of a Lambert or a Lady Fairfax. But his morality and his manners are misplaced in Illyria. He is opposed to the proper *levities* of the piece, and falls in the unequal contest. Still his pride, or his gravity, (call it which you will,) is inherent, and native to the man, not mock or affected, which latter only are the fit objects to excite laughter. His quality is at the best unlovely, but neither buffoon nor contemptible. His bearing is lofty, a little above his station, but probably not much above his deserts. We see no reason why he should not have been brave, honourable, accomplished. His careless committal of the ring to the ground (which he was commissioned to restore to Cesario) bespeaks a generosity of birth and feeling. His dialect on all occasions is that of a gentleman and a man of education. We must not confound him with the eternal old, low steward of comedy. He is master of the household to a great princess; a dignity probably conferred upon him for other respects than age or length of service. Olivia, at the first indication of his supposed madness, declares that she "would not have him miscarry for half of her dowry." Does this look as if the character was meant to appear little or insignificant? Once, indeed, she accuses him to his face—of what?—of being "sick of self-love,"—but with a gentleness and considerateness which could not have been if she had not thought that this particular infirmity shaded some virtues. His rebuke to the knight and his sottish revellers is sensible and spirited; and when we take into consideration the unprotected condition of his mistress, and the strict regard with which her state of real or dissembled mourning would draw the eyes of the world upon her house-affairs, Malvolio might feel the honour of the family in some sort in his keeping; as it appears not that Olivia had any more brothers or kinsmen to look to it—for Sir Toby had dropped all such nice respects at the buttery-hatch. That Malvolio was meant to be represented as possessing estimable qualities, the expression of the Duke, in his anxiety to have him reconciled, almost infers: "Pursue him, and entreat him to a peace." Even in his abused state of chains and darkness, a sort of greatness seems never to desert him. He argues highly and well with the supposed Sir Topas, and philosophises gallantly upon his straw.[1] There must have been some shadow of worth about the man; he must have been something more than a mere vapour—a thing of straw, or Jack in office—before Fabian and Maria could have ventured sending him upon a courting errand to Olivia. There was some consonancy (as he would say) in the undertaking, or the jest would have been too bold even for that house of misrule.

Bensley, accordingly, threw over the part an air of Spanish loftiness. He looked, spake, and moved like an old Castilian. He was starch,

---

[1] *Clown.* What is the opinion of Pythagoras concerning wild fowl?
Mal. That the soul of our grandam might haply inhabit a bird.
Clown. What thinkest thou of his opinion?
Mal. I think nobly of the soul, and no way approve his opinion.

spruce, opinionated, but his superstructure of pride seemed bottomed upon a sense of worth. There was something in it beyond the coxcomb. It was big and swelling, but you could not be sure that it was hollow. You might wish to see it taken down, but you felt that it was upon an elevation. He was magnificent from the out-set; but when the decent sobrieties of the cha racter began to give way, and the poison of self-love, in his conceit of the Countess's affec-tion, gradually to work, you would have thought that the hero of La Mancha in person stood before you. How he went smiling to himself! With what ineffable carelessness would he twirl his gold chain! What a dream it was! You were infected with the illusion, and did not wish that it should be removed. You had no room for laughter. If an unseason-able reflection of morality obtruded itself, it was a deep sense of the pitiable infirmity of man's nature, that can lay him open to such frenzies; but, in truth, you rather admired than pitied the lunacy while it lasted; you felt that an hour of such mistake was worth an age with the eyes open. Who would not wish to live but for a day in the conceit of such a lady's love as Olivia? Why, the Duke would have given his principality but for a quarter of a minute, sleeping or waking, to have been so deluded. The man seemed to tread upon air, to taste manna, to walk with his head in the clouds, to mate Hyperion. O shake not the castles of his

pride; endure yet for a season bright moments
of confidence; "stand still, ye watches of the
element," that Malvolio may be still in fancy
fair Olivia's lord!—but fate and retribution say
"no." I hear the mischievous titter of Maria—
the witty taunts of Sir Toby—the still more in-
supportable triumph of the foolish knight—the
counterfeit Sir Topas is unmasked—and "thus
the whirligig of time," as the true clown hath
it, "brings in his revenges." I confess that I
never saw the catastrophe of this character,
while Bensley played it, without a kind of
tragic interest. There was good foolery too.
Few now remember Dodd. What an Aguecheek
the stage lost in him! Lovegrove, who came
nearest to the old actors, revived the character
some few seasons ago, and made it sufficiently
grotesque; but Dodd was *it,* as it came out of
Nature's hands. It might be said to remain *in
puris naturalibus.* In expressing slowness of
apprehension, this actor surpassed all others.
You could see the first dawn of an idea stealing
slowly over his countenance, climbing up by
little and little, with a painful process, till it
cleared up at last to the fulness of a twilight
conception—its highest meridian. He seemed
to keep back his intellect, as some have had the
power to retard their pulsation. The balloon
takes less time in filling than it took to cover
the expansion of his broad moony face over all
its quarters with expression. A glimmer of understanding would appear in a corner of his

eye, and for lack of fuel go out again. A part of his forehead would catch a little intelligence, and be a long time in communicating it to the remainder.

I am ill at dates, but I think it is now better than five-and-twenty years ago, that walking in the gardens of Gray's Inn,—they were then far finer than they are now; the accursed Verulam Buildings had not encroached upon all the east side of them, cutting out delicate green crankles, and shouldering away one of two of the stately alcoves of the terrace—the survivor stands gaping and relationless as if it remembered its brother—they are still the best gardens of any of the Inns of Court, my beloved Temple not forgotten—have the gravest character; their aspect being altogether reverend and law-breathing; Bacon has left the impress of his foot upon their gravel walks;—taking my afternoon solace on a Summer day upon the aforesaid terrace, a comely sad personage came towards me, whom, from his grave air and deportment, I judged to be one of the old Benchers of the Inn. He had a serious, thoughtful forehead, and seemed to be in meditations of mortality. As I have an instinctive awe of old Benchers, I was passing him with that sort of sub-indicative token of respect which one is apt to demonstrate towards a venerable stranger, and which rather denotes an inclination to greet him, than any positive motion of the body to that effect, (a species of humility and will-worship which I observe, nine times out of ten, rather puzzles than pleases the person it is offered to,) when the face, turning full upon me, strangely identified itself with that of Dodd. Upon close inspection I was not mistaken. But could this sad thoughtful countenance be the same vacant face of folly which I had hailed so often under circumstances of gaiety; which I had never seen without a smile, or recognised but as the usher of mirth; that looked out so formally flat in Foppington, so frothily pert in Tattle, so impotently busy in Backbite; so blankly divested of all meaning, or resolutely expressive of none, in Acres, in Fribble, and a thousand agreeable impertinences? Was this the face, full of thought and carefulness, that had so often divested itself at will of every trace of either to give me diversion, to clear my cloudy face for two or three hours at least of its furrows? Was this the face—manly, sober, intelligent—which I had so often despised, made mocks at, made merry with? The remembrance of the freedoms which I had taken with it came upon me with a reproach of insult. I could have asked it pardon. I thought it looked upon me with a sense of injury. There is something strange as well as sad in seeing actors, your pleasant fellows particularly, subjected to and suffering the common lot; their fortunes, their casualties, their deaths, seem to belong to the scene, their actions to be amenable to poetic justice only.

We can hardly connect them with more awful responsibilities. The death of this fine actor took place shortly after this meeting. He had quitted the stage some months; and, as I learned afterwards, had been in the habit of resorting daily to these gardens, almost to the day of his decease. In these serious walks, probably, he was divesting himself of many scenic and some real vanities—weaning himself from the frivolities of the lesser and the greater theatre—doing gentle penance for a life of no very reprehensible fooleries—taking off by degrees the buffoon mask, which he might feel he had worn too long—and rehearsing for a more solemn cast of part. Dying, he "put on the weeds of Dominic."[1]

If few can remember Dodd, many yet living will not easily forget the pleasant creature who in those days enacted the part of the

---

[1] Dodd was a man of reading, and left at his death a choice collection of old English literature. I should judge him to have been a man of wit. I know one instance of an impromptu which no length of study could have bettered. My merry friend, Jem White, had seen Dodd one evening in Aguecheek, and recognising him the next day in Fleet Street, was irresistibly impelled to take off his hat and salute him as the identical Knight of the preceding evening with a "Save you, *Sir Andrew.*" Dodd, not at all disconcerted at this unusual address from a stranger, with a courteous half-rebuking wave of the hand, put him off with an "Away, *Fool!*"

Charles Lamb

Clown to Dodd's Sir Andrew. Richard, or
rather Dicky Suett—for so in his life-time he
delighted to be called, and time hath ratified
the appellation—lieth buried on the north side
of the cemetery of Holy Paul, to whose service his nonage and tender years were dedicated. There are who do yet remember him
at that period—his pipe clear and harmonious.
He would often speak of his chorister days,
when he was "cherub Dicky."

What clipped his wings, or made it expedient that he should exchange the holy for the
profane state; whether he had lost his good
voice, (his best recommendation to that office,)
like Sir John, "with hallooing and singing of
anthems;" or whether he was adjudged to
lack something, even in those early years of
the gravity indispensable to an occupation
which professeth to "commerce with the skies,"
—I could never rightly learn; but we find him
after the probation of a twelvemonth or so, re-
verting to a secular condition, and become one
of us.

I think he was not altogether of that timber
out of which cathedral seats and sounding-
boards are hewed. But if a glad heart—kind,
and therefore glad—be any part of sanctity,
then might the robe of motley, with which he
invested himself with so much humility after
his deprivation, and which he wore so long
with so much blameless satisfaction to himself

and to the public, be accepted for a surplice—
his white stole, and *albe*.

The first-fruits of his secularisation was an
engagement upon the boards of Old Drury, at
which theatre he commenced, as I have been
told, with adopting the manner of Parsons in
old men's characters. At the period in which
most of us knew him, he was no more an imi-
tator than he was in any true sense himself
imitable.

He was the Robin Goodfellow of the stage.
He came in to trouble all things with a welcome perplexity, himself no whit troubled for
the matter. He was known, like Puck, by his
note—*Ha! Ha! Ha!*— sometimes deepening
to *Ho! Ho! Ho!* with an irresistible accession, derived, perhaps, remotely from his ec-
clesiastical education, foreign to his prototype
of—*O La!* Thousands of hearts yet respond
to the chuckling *O La!* of Dicky Suett,
brought back to their remembrance by the
faithful transcript of his friend Mathew's mim-
icry. The "force of nature could no further
go." He drolled upon the stock of these two
syllables richer than the cuckoo.

Care, that troubles all the world, was forgotten in his composition. Had he had but
two grains (nay, half a grain) of it, he could
never have supported himself upon those two
spider's strings, which served him (in the latter part of his unmixed existence) as legs. A
doubt or a scruple must have made him totter,

Charles Lamb

a sigh have puffed him down; the weight of a frown had staggered him, a wrinkle made him lose his balance. But on he went, scrambling upon those airy stilts of his, with Robin Goodfellow, "through brake, through briar," reckless of a scratched face or a torn doublet.

Shakespeare foresaw him, when he framed his fools and jesters. They have all the true Suett stamp, a loose and shambling gait, a slippery tongue, this last the ready midwife to a without-pain-delivered jest; in words, light as air, venting truths deep as the centre; with idlest rhymes tagging conceit when busiest, singing with Lear in the Tempest, or Sir Toby at the buttery-hatch.

Jack Bannister and he had the fortune to be more of personal favourites with the town than any actors before or after. The difference, I take it, was this:—Jack was more *beloved* for his sweet, good-natured, moral pretensions. Dicky was more *liked* for his sweet, good-natured, no pretensions at all. Your whole conscience stirred with Bannister's performance of Walter in the *Children in the Wood;* but Dicky seemed like a thing, as Shakspeare says of Love, too young to know what conscience is. He put us into Vesta's days. Evil fled before him—not as from Jack, as from an antagonist,—but because it could not touch him, any more than a cannon ball a fly. He was delivered from the burthen of that death; and, when Death came himself,

66

not in metaphor, to fetch Dicky, it is recorded
of him by Robert Palmer, who kindly watched
his exit, that he received the last stroke, neither
varying his accustomed tranquillity, nor tune,
with the simple exclamation, worthy to have
been recorded in his epitaph—*O La! O La!
Bobby!*

The elder Palmer (of stage-treading celeb-
rity) commonly played Sir Toby in those days;
but there is a solidity of wit in the jests of
that half-Falstaff which he did not quite fill
out. He was as much too showy as Moody
(who sometimes took the part) was dry and
sottish. In sock or buskin there was an air
of swaggering gentility about Jack Palmer. He
was a *gentleman* with a slight infusion of *the
footman.* His brother Bob (of recenter memory,) who was his shadow in everything while
he lived, and dwindled into less than a shadow
afterwards, was a *gentleman* with a little
stronger infusion of the *latter ingredient;* that
was all. It is amazing how a little of the more
or less makes a difference in these things.
When you saw Bobby in the Duke's Servant,[1]
you said "What a pity such a pretty fellow
was only a servant!" When you saw Jack
figuring in Captain Absolute, you thought you
could trace his promotion to some lady of
quality who fancied the handsome fellow in
his topknot, and had bought him a commis-

----

[1] *High Life Below Stairs.*

Charles Lamb

sion. Therefore Jack in Dick Amlet was insuperable.

Jack had two voices, both plausible, hypocritical, and insinuating; but his secondary or supplemental voice still more decisively histrionic than his common one. It was reserved for the spectator; and the dramatis personæ were supposed to know nothing at all about it. The *lies* of Young Wilding, and the *sentiments* in Joseph Surface, were thus marked out in a sort of italics to the audience. This secret correspondence with the company before the curtain (which is the bane and death of tragedy) has an extremely happy effect in some kinds of comedy, in the more highly artificial comedy of Congreve or of Sheridan especially, where the absolute sense of reality (so indispensable to scenes of interest) is not required, or would rather interfere to diminish your pleasure. The fact is, you do not believe in such characters as Surface—the villain of artificial comedy—even while you read or see them. If you did, they would shock and not divert you. When Ben, in *Love for Love,* returns from sea, the following exquisite dialogue occurs at his first meeting with his father:—

Sir Sampson. Thou hast been many a weary league, Ben, since I saw thee.

Ben. Ey, ey, been? Been far enough, and that be all. Well, father, and how do all at home? How does brother Dick, and brother Val?

Sir Sampson. Dick! body o' me, Dick has

been dead these two years. I writ you word
when you were at Leghorn.

Ben. Mess, that's true: marry, I had forgot. Dick is dead, as you say. Well, and
how, I have a many questions to ask you.

Here is an instance of insensibility which in
real life would be revolting, or rather in real
life could not have co-existed with the warm-
hearted temperament of the character. But
when you read it in the spirit with which such
playful selections and specious combinations
rather than strict *metaphrases* of nature should
be taken, or when you saw Bannister play it, it
neither did, nor does, wound the moral sense
at all. For what is Ben—the pleasant sailor
which Bannister gives us—but a piece of satire
—a creation of Congreve's fancy—a dreamy
combination of all the accidents of a sailor's
character—his contempt of money—his credu-
lity to women—with that necessary estrange-
ment from home which it is just within the
verge of credibility to suppose *might* produce
such an hallucination as is here described. We
never think the worse of Ben for it, or feel it
as a stain upon his character. But when an
actor comes, and instead of the delightful phantom—the creature dear to half-belief, which
Bannister exhibited—displays before our eyes
a downright concretion of a Wapping sailor, a
jolly warm-hearted Jack Tar, and nothing else;
when instead of investing it with a delicious
confusedness of the head, and a veering undi-

rected goodness of purpose, he gives to it a downright daylight understanding, and a full consciousness of its actions; thrusting forward the sensibilities of the character with a pretence as if it stood upon nothing else, and was to be judged by them alone—we feel the discord of the thing; the scene is disturbed; a real man has got in among the dramatis personæ, and puts them out. We want the sailor turned out. We feel that his true place is not behind the curtain, but in the first or second gallery.

DETACHED THOUGHTS ON BOOKS AND READING

To mind the inside of a book is to entertain one's self with the forced product of another man's brain. Now I think a man of quality and breeding may be much amused with the natural sprouts of his own.—*Lord Foppington, in the Relapse.*

AN ingenious acquaintance of my own was so much struck with this bright sally of his Lordship, that he has left off reading altogether, to the great improvement of his originality. At the hazard of losing some credit on this head, I must confess that I dedicate no inconsiderable portion of my time to other people's thoughts. I dream away my life in others' speculations. I love to lose myself in other men's minds. When I am not walking I am reading; I cannot sit and think. Books think for me.

I have no repugnances. Shaftesbury is not too genteel for me, nor Jonathan Wild too low. I can read anything which I call *a book*. There are things in that shape which I cannot allow for such.

In this catalogue of *books which are no books—biblia a-biblia,* I reckon Court Calendars, Directories, Pocket Books, Draught Boards bound and lettered on the back, Scientific Treatises, Almanacks, Statutes at Large: the works of Hume, Gibbon, Robertson, Beattie, Soame Jenyns, and generally all those volumes which "no gentleman's library should be without:" the Histories of Flavius Josephus (that learned Jew), and Paley's Moral Philosophy. With these exceptions I can read almost anything. I bless my stars for a taste so catholic, so unexcluding.

I confess that it moves my spleen to see these *things in books' clothing* perched upon shelves, like false saints, usurpers of true shrines, intruders into the sanctuary, thrusting out the legitimate occupants. To reach down a well-bound semblance of a volume, and hope it some kind-hearted play-book, then, opening what "seem its leaves," to come bolt upon a withering Population Essay. To expect a Steele or a Farquhar, and find Adam Smith. To view a well-arranged assortment of block-headed Encyclopædias (Anglicanas or Metropolitanas) set out in an array of russia or morocco, when a tithe of that good leather would comfortably

re-clothe my shivering folios—would renovate
Paracelsus himself, and enable old Raymund
Lully to look like himself again in the world.
I never see these impostors but I long to strip
them, to warm my ragged veterans in their
spoils.

To be strong-backed and neat-bound is the
desideratum of a volume. Magnificence comes
after. This, when it can be afforded, is not to
be lavished upon all kinds of books indiscrimi-
nately. For instance, I would not dress a set
of Magazines in full suit. The dishabille, or
half binding, (with russia backs ever,) is *our*
costume. A Shakspeare or a Milton (unless
the first editions) it were mere foppery to trick
out in gay apparel. The possession of them
confers no distinction. The exterior of them
(the things themselves being so common),
strange to say, raises no sweet emotions, no
tickling sense of property in the owner. Thomson's Seasons, again, looks best (I maintain it)
a little torn and dog's-eared. How beautiful
to a genuine lover of reading are the sullied
leaves and worn-out appearance, nay, the very
odour, (beyond russia,) if we would not forget kind feelings in fastidiousness, of an old
" Circulating Library " Tom Jones, or Vicar of
Wakefield ! How they speak of the thousand
thumbs that have turned over their pages with
delight ! of the lone sempstress, whom they
may have cheered (milliner, or harder-work-
ing mantuamaker) after her long day's needle-

tool, running far into midnight, when she has
snatched an hour, ill spared from sleep, to
steep her cares, as in some Lethean cup, in
spelling out their enchanting contents! Who
would have them a whit less soiled? What
better condition could we desire to see them in?

In some respects the better a book is, the
less it demands from binding. Fielding, Smollett, Sterne, and all that class of perpetually
self-reproductive volumes — Great Nature's
Stereotypes—we see them individually perish
with less regret, because we know the copies
of them to be "eterne." But where a book is
at once both good and rare, where the individual is almost the species, and when *that* per-
ishes,

We know not where is that Promethean torch
That can its light relumine;

such a book, for instance, as the Life of the
Duke of Newcastle, by his Duchess: no casket
is rich enough, no casing sufficiently durable,
to honour and keep safe such a jewel.

Not only rare volumes of this description,
which seem hopeless ever to be reprinted, but
old editions of writers, such as Sir Philip Syd-
ney, Bishop Taylor, Milton in his prose works,
Fuller, (of whom we *have* reprints, yet the
books themselves, though they go about, and
are talked of here and there, we know have not
endenizened themselves, nor possibly ever will,
in the national heart, so as to become stock

books,) it is good to possess these in durable and costly covers. I do not care for a First Folio of Shakspeare. I rather prefer the common editions of Rowe and Tonson, without notes, and with *plates*, which, being so execrably bad, serve as maps or modest remembrancers to the text; and without pretending to any supposable emulation with it, are so much better than the Shakspeare *engravings*, which *did*. I have a community of feeling with my countryman about his Plays, and I like those editions of him best which have been oftenest tumbled about and handled. On the contrary, I cannot read Beaumont and Fletcher but in Folio. The Octavo editions are painful to look at. I have no sympathy with them. If they were as much read as the current editions of the other poet, I should prefer them in that shape to the older one. I do not know a more heartless sight than the reprint of the " Anatomy of Melancholy." What need was there of unearthing the bones of that fantastic old great man, to expose them in a winding-sheet of the newest fashion to modern censure? What hapless stationer could dream of Burton ever becoming popular? The wretched Malone could not do worse, when he bribed the sexton of Stratford Church to let him white-wash the painted effigy of old Shakspeare, which stood there, in rude but lively fashion depicted, to the very colour of the cheek, the eye, the eyebrow, hair, the very dress he used to wear,

—the only authentic testimony we had, however imperfect, of these curious parts and parcels of him. They covered him over with a coat of white paint. By——, if I had been a justice of peace for Warwickshire, I would have clapped both commentator and sexton fast in the stocks, for a pair of meddling sacrilegious varlets.

I think I see them at their work, these sapient trouble-tombs!

Shall I be thought fantastical if I confess that the names of some of our poets sound sweeter, and have a finer relish to the ear, (to mine at least,) than that of Milton or of Shakspeare? It may be that the latter are more staled and rung upon in common discourse. The sweetest names, and which carry a perfume in the mention, are Kit Marlowe, Drayton, Drummond of Hawthornden, and Cowley.

Much depends upon *when* and *where* you read a book. In the five or six impatient minutes before the dinner is quite ready, who would think of taking up the "Fairy Queen" for a stop-gap, or a volume of Bishop Andrewes's sermons?

Milton almost requires a solemn service of music to be played before you enter upon him. But he brings his music; to which, who listens, had need bring docile thoughts and purged ears.

Winter evenings—the world shut out—with less of ceremony the gentle Shakspeare enters.

Charles Lamb

At such a season the *Tempest*, or his own *Winter's Tale*.

These two poets you cannot avoid reading aloud—to yourself, or (as it chances) to some single person listening. More than one, and it degenerates into an audience.

Books of quick interest, that hurry on for incidents, are for the eye to glide over only. It will not do to read them out. I could never listen to even the better kind of modern novels without extreme irksomeness.

A newspaper read out is intolerable. In some of the Bank offices it is the custom (to save so much individual time) for one of the clerks, who is the best scholar, to commence upon the *Times*, or the *Chronicle*, and recite its entire contents aloud, *pro bono publico*. With every advantage of lungs and elocution, the effect is singularly vapid. In barbers' shops and public-houses a fellow will get up and spell out a paragraph, which he communicates as some discovery. Another follows with *his* selection. So the entire journal transpires at length by piece-meal. Seldom-readers are slow readers, and without this expedient no one in the company would probably ever travel through the contents of a whole paper.

Newspapers always excite curiosity. No one ever lays one down without a feeling of disappointment.

What an eternal time that gentleman in black, at Nando's, keeps the paper! I am sick of hearing the waiter bawling out incessantly, "The *Chronicle* is in hand, Sir."

Coming into an inn at night—having ordered your supper—what can be more delightful than to find lying in the window-seat, left there time out of mind by the carelessness of some former guest, two or three numbers of the old *Town and Country Magazine,* with its amusing *tête-à-tête* pictures—"The Royal Lover and Lady G——;" "The Melting Platonic and the old Beau,"—and such-like antiquated scandal? Would you exchange it—at that time, and in that place—for a better book?

Poor Tobin, who latterly fell blind, did not regret it so much for the weightier kinds of reading, (the "Paradise Lost," or "Comus," he could have *read* to him,) but he missed the pleasure of skimming over with his own eye a magazine, or a light pamphlet.

I should not care to be caught in the serious avenues of some cathedral alone, and reading *Candide.*

I do not remember a more whimsical surprise than having been once detected, by a familiar damsel, reclined at my ease upon the grass, on Primrose Hill, (her Cythera,) reading *Pamela.* There was nothing in the book to make a man seriously ashamed at the exposure; but as she seated herself down by me, and seemed determined to read in company, I could have wished it had been any other book. We read on very sociably for a few pages; but not finding the author much to her taste she got up and went away. Gentle casuist, I leave it to thee to conjecture, whether the blush (for there was one between us) was the property of the nymph or the swain in this dilemma. From me you shall never get the secret.

I am not much a friend to out-of-doors reading. I cannot settle my spirits to it. I knew a Unitarian minister, who was generally to be seen upon Snow Hill, (as yet Skinner's Street *was not,*) between the hours of ten and eleven in the morning, studying a volume of Lardner. I own this to have been a strain of abstraction beyond my reach. I used to admire how he sidled along, keeping clear of secular contacts. An illiterate encounter with a porter's knot or a bread-basket would have quickly put to flight all the theology I am master of, and have left me worse than indifferent to the five points.

There is a class of street readers whom I can never contemplate without affection,—the poor gentry, who, not having wherewithal to buy or hire a book, filch a little learning at the open stalls; the owner, with his hard eye, casting envious looks at them all the while, and thinking when they will have done. Venturing tenderly, page after page, expecting every moment when he shall interpose his interdict, and yet unable to deny themselves the gratification, they "snatch a fearful joy." Martin B——, in this way, by daily fragments, got through two volumes of "Clarissa," when the stall-keeper

Essays

damped his laudable ambition, by asking him
(it was in his younger days) whether he meant
to purchase the work. M—— declares, that under no circumstance in his life did he ever pe-
ruse a book with half the satisfaction which he
took in those uneasy snatches. A quaint poetess
of our day has moralised upon this subject in
two very touching but homely stanzas :—

" I saw a boy with eager eye
Open a book upon a stall,
And read, as he'd devour it all ;
Which when the stall-man did espy,
Soon to the boy I heard him call,
' You Sir, you never buy a book,
Therefore in one you shall not look.'
The boy pass'd slowly on, and with a sigh
He wish'd he never had been taught to read,
Then of the old churl's books he should have
    had no need.

Of sufferings the poor have many,
Which never can the rich annoy :
I soon perceived another boy,
Who look'd as if he had not any
Food—for that day at least—enjoy
The sight of cold meat in a tavern larder.
This boy's case, then thought I, is surely
    harder,
Thus hungry, longing, thus without a penny,
Beholding choice of dainty-dressed meat :
No wonder if he wish he ne'er had learn'd to
    eat."

Charles Lamb

THE SUPERANNUATED MAN

Sera tamen respexit.
Libertas.   VIRGIL.

A Clerk I was in London gay.—O'KEEFE.

IF peradventure, Reader, it has been thy lot
to waste the golden years of thy life, thy shining youth, in the irksome confinement of an
office; to have thy prison days prolonged
through middle age down to decrepitude and
silver hairs, without hope of release or respite;
to have lived to forget that there are such
things as holidays, or to remember them but
as the prerogatives of childhood; then, and
then only, will you be able to appreciate my
deliverance.

It is now six-and-thirty years since I took
my seat at the desk in Mincing Lane. Melancholy was the transition at fourteen from the
abundant playtime, and the frequently inter-
vening vacations of school days, to the eight,
nine, and sometimes ten hours a-day attendance at the counting-house. But time partially
reconciles us to anything. I gradually became
content; doggedly contented, as wild animals
in cages.

It is true I had my Sundays to myself; but
Sundays, admirable as the institution of them
is for purposes of worship, are for that very
reason the very worst adapted for days of unbending and recreation. In particular, there is

a gloom for me attendant upon a City Sunday,
a weight in the air. I miss the cheerful cries of
London, the music, and the ballad-singers, the
buzz and stirring murmur of the streets. Those
eternal bells depress me. The closed shops repel me. Prints, pictures, all the glittering and
endless succession of knacks and gew-gaws,
and ostentatiously displayed wares of tradesmen, which make a week-day saunter through
the less busy parts of the metropolis so delightful, are shut out. No book-stalls deli-
ciously to idle over; no busy faces to recreate
the idle man who contemplates them ever passing by; the very face of business a charm by
contrast to his temporary relaxation from it.
Nothing to be seen but unhappy countenances
—or half-happy at best—of emancipated 'pren-
tices and little tradesfolk, with here and there
a servant-maid that has got leave to go out,
who, slaving all the week, with the habit has
lost almost the capacity of enjoying a free
hour, and livelily expressing the hollowness of
a day's pleasuring. The very strollers in the
fields on that day look anything but comfortable.

But besides Sundays, I had a day at Easter
and a day at Christmas, with a full week in the
Summer to go and air myself in my native
fields of Hertfordshire. This last was a great
indulgence; and the prospect of its recurrence,
I believe, alone kept me up through the year,
and made my durance tolerable. But when the

week came round, did the glittering phantom of the distance keep touch with me? or rather was it not a series of seven uneasy days, spent in restless pursuit of pleasure, and a wearisome anxiety to find out how to make the most of them? Where was the quiet? where the promised rest? Before I had a taste of it, it was vanished. I was at the desk again, counting upon the fifty-one tedious weeks that must intervene before such another snatch would come. Still the prospect of its coming threw something of an illumination upon the darker side of my captivity. Without it, as I have said, I could scarcely have sustained my thraldom.

Independently of the rigours of attendance, I have ever been haunted with a sense (perhaps a mere caprice) of incapacity for business. This, during my latter years, had increased to such a degree that it was visible in all the lines of my countenance. My health and my good spirits flagged. I had perpetually a dread of some crisis, to which I should be found unequal. Besides my daylight servitude, I served over again all night in my sleep, and would awake with terrors of imaginary false entries, errors in my accounts, and the like. I was fifty years of age, and no prospect of emancipation presented itself. I had grown to my desk, as it were; and the wood had entered into my soul.

My fellows in the office would sometimes rally me upon the trouble legible in my countenance; but I did not know that it had raised the suspicions of any of my employers, when, on the fifth of last month, a day ever to be remembered by me, L——, the junior partner in the firm, calling me on one side, directly taxed me with my bad looks, and frankly inquired the cause of them. So taxed, I honestly made confession of my infirmity, and added that I was afraid I should eventually be obliged to resign his service. He spoke some words of course to hearten me, and there the matter rested. A whole week I remained labouring under the impression that I had acted imprudently in my disclosure; that I had foolishly given a handle against myself, and had been anticipating my own dismissal. A week passed in this manner, the most anxious one, I verily believe, in my whole life, when on the evening of the 12th of April, just as I was about quiting my desk to go home, (it might be about eight o'clock,) I received an awful summons to attend the presence of the whole assembled firm in the formidable back parlour. I thought now my time was surely come. I have done for myself. I am going to be told that they have no longer occasion for me. L——, I could see, smiled at the terror I was in, which was a little relief to me,—when to my utter astonishment B——, the eldest partner, began a formal harangue to me on the length of my services, my very meritorious conduct during the whole of the time, (the deuce, thought I, how did he find out that? I protest I never had the con-

Charles Lamb

fidence to think as much). He went on to descant on the expediency of retiring at a certain time of life, (how my heart panted!) and asking me a few questions as to the amount of my own property, of which I have a little, ended with a proposal, to which his three partners nodded a grave assent, that I should accept from the house, which I had served so well, a pension for life to the amount of two-thirds of my accustomed salary,—a magnificent offer! I do not know what I answered between surprise and gratitude, but it was understood that I accepted their proposal, and I was told that I was free from that hour to leave their service. I stammered out a bow, and at just ten minutes after eight I went home—forever. This noble benefit (gratitude forbids me to conceal their names) I owe to the kindness of the most munificent firm in the world,—the house of Boldero, Merryweather, Bosanquet, and Lacy.

Esto perpetua!

For the first day or two I felt stunned, overwhelmed. I could only apprehend my felicity; I was too confused to taste it sincerely. I wandered about, thinking I was happy, and knowing that I was not. I was in the condition of a prisoner in the old Bastile, suddenly let loose after a forty years' confinement. I could scarce trust myself with myself. It was like passing out of Time into Eternity, for it is

Essays

a sort of Eternity for a man to have his Time all to himself. It seemed to me that I had more time on my hands than I could ever manage. From a poor man, poor in Time, I was suddenly lifted up into a vast revenue; I could see no end of my possessions: I wanted some steward, or judicious bailiff, to manage my estates in Time for me. And here let me caution persons grown old in active business, not lightly, nor without weighing their own resources, to forego their customary employment all at once, for there may be danger in it. I feel it by myself, but I know that my resources are sufficient; and now that those first giddy raptures have subsided, I have a quiet home feeling of the blessedness of my condition. I am in no hurry. Having all holidays, I am as though I had none. If Time hung heavy upon me, I could walk it away; but I do *not* walk all day long, as I used to do in those transient holidays, thirty miles a day, to make the most of them. If Time were troublesome, I could read it away; but I do *not* read in that violent measure, with which, having no Time my own but candlelight Time, I used to weary out my head and eyesight in by-gone Winters. I walk, read, or scribble, (as now,) just when the fit seizes me. I no longer hunt after pleasure; I let it come to me. I am like the man

————that's born, and has his years come to
  him,
In some green desert.

Charles Lamb

"Years!" you will say; what is that super-annuated simpleton calculating upon? He has already told us he is past fifty."

I have indeed lived nominally fifty years; but deduct out of them the hours which I have lived to other people, and not to myself, and you will find me still a young fellow: for *that* is the only true Time which a man can properly call his own, that which he has all to himself; the rest, though in some sense he may be said to live it, is other people's Time, not his. The remnant of my poor days, long or short, is at least multiplied for me threefold. My ten next years, if I stretch so far, will be as long as any preceding thirty. 'Tis a fair Rule-of-Three sum.

Among the strange fantasies which beset me at the commencement of my freedom, and of which all traces are not yet gone, one was, that a vast tract of time that intervened since I quitted the Counting House. I could not conceive of it as an affair of yesterday. The partners and the clerks, with whom I had for so many years and for so many hours in each day of the year been closely associated, being suddenly removed from them, they seemed as dead to me. There is a fine passage, which may serve to illustrate this fancy, in a Tragedy by Sir Robert Howard, speaking of a friend's death:—

————'Twas but just now he went away;
I have not since had time to shed a tear;

And yet the distance does the same appear
As if he had been a thousand years from me!
Time takes no measure in Eternity.

To dissipate this awkward feeling, I have
been fain to go among them once or twice
since; to visit my old desk-fellows—my co-
brethren of the quill—that I had left below in
the state militant. Not all the kindness with
which they received me could quite restore to
me that pleasant familiarity which I had
hitherto enjoyed among them. We cracked
some of our old jokes, but methought they
went off but faintly. My old desk, the peg
where I hung my hat, were appropriated to another. I knew it must be, but I could not take
it kindly. D——l take me, if I did not feel
some remorse—beast, if I had not—at quitting
my old compeers, the faithful partners of my
toils for six-and-thirty years, that smoothed
for me with their jokes and conundrums the
ruggedness of my professional road. Had it
been so rugged then, after all? or was I simply a coward? Well, it is too late to repent; and
I also know that these suggestions are a common
fallacy of the mind on such occasions. But my
heart smote me. I had violently broken the
bands betwixt us. It was at least not courteous.
I shall be some time before I get quite reconciled to the separation. Farewell, old cronies;
yet not for long, for again and again I will
come among ye, if I shall have your leave.
Farewell, Ch——, dry, sarcastic, and friendly!

Charles Lamb

Do——, mild, slow to move, and gentlemanly!
Pl——, officious to do and to volunteer good
services!—and thou, thou dreary pile, fit mansion for a Gresham or a Whittington of old,
stately house of Merchants; with thy labyrin-
thine passages, and light-excluding, pent-up offices, where candles for one-half the year supplied the place of the sun's light; unhealthy
contributor to my weal, stern fosterer of my
living, farewell! In thee remain, and not in
the obscure collection of some wandering bookseller, my "works!" There let them rest, as
I do from my labours, piled on thy massy
shelves, more MSS. in folio than ever Aquinas
left, and full as useful! My mantle I be-
queathe among ye.

A fortnight has passed since the date of my
first communication. At that period I was approaching to tranquillity, but had not reached
it. I boasted of a calm indeed, but it was com-
parative only. Something of the first flutter
was left; an unsettling sense of novelty; the
dazzle to weak eyes of unaccustomed light. I
missed my old chains, forsooth, as if they had
been some necessary part of my apparel. I
was a poor Carthusian, from strict cellular discipline suddenly by some revolution returned
upon the world. I am now as if I had never
been other than my own master. It is natural
to me to go where I please, to do what I please.
I find myself at eleven o'clock in the day in
Bond Street, and it seems to me that I have

been sauntering there at that very hour for years past. I digress into Soho, to explore a bookstall. Methinks I have been thirty years a collector. There is nothing strange nor new in it. I find myself before a fine picture in the morning. Was it ever otherwise? What is become of Fish Street Hill? Where is Fenchurch Street? Stones of old Mincing Lane, which I have worn with my daily pilgrimage for six-and-thirty years, to the footsteps of what toil-worn clerk are your everlasting flints now vocal? I indent the gayer flags of Pall Mall. It is 'Change time, and I am strangely among the Elgin marbles. It was no hyperbole when I ventured to compare the change in my condition to a passing into another world. Time stands still in a manner to me. I have lost all distinction of season. I do not know the day of the week or of the month. Each day used to be individually felt by me in its reference to the foreign post days; in its distance from, or propinquity to, the next Sunday. I had my Wednesday feelings, my Saturday nights' sensations. The genius of each day was upon me distinctly during the whole of it, affecting my appetite, spirits, &c. The phantom of the next day, with the dreary five to follow, sate as a load upon my poor Sabbath recreations. What charm has washed that Ethiop white? What is gone of Black Monday? All days are the same. Sunday itself—that unfortunate failure of a holiday, as it too often

proved, what with my sense of its fugitiveness,
and over-care to get the greatest quantity of
pleasure out of it—is melted down into a week-
day. I can spare time to go to church now,
without grudging the huge cantle which it
used to seem to cut out of the holiday. I have
time for everything. I can visit a sick friend.
I can interrupt the man of much occupation
when he is busiest. I can insult over him
with an invitation to take a day's pleasure with
me to Windsor this fine May morning. It is
Lucretian pleasure to behold the poor drudges,
whom I have left behind in the world, carking
and caring; like horses in a mill, drudging on
in the same eternal round: and what is it all
for? A man can never have too much Time
to himself, nor too little to do. Had I a little
son, I would christen him NOTHING-TO-DO; he
should do nothing. Man, I verily believe, is
out of his element as long as he is operative.
I am altogether for the life contemplative. Will
no kindly earthquake come and swallow up
those accursed cotton mills? Take me that
lumber of a desk there, and bowl it down

As low as to the fiends.

I am no longer******, clerk to the Firm
of, &c. I am Retired Leisure. I am to be met
with in trim gardens. I am already come to be
known by my vacant face and careless gesture,
perambulating at no fixed place, nor with any
settled purpose. I walk about; not to and

from. They tell me, a certain *cum dignitate* air, that has been buried so long with my other good parts, has begun to shoot forth in my person. I perceptibly grow into gentility. When I take up a newspaper, it is to read the state of the opera. *Opus operatum est.* I have done all that I came into this world to do. I have worked task-work, and have the rest of the day to myself.

OLD CHINA

I HAVE an almost feminine partiality for old china. When I go to see any great house I inquire for the china closet, and next for the picture gallery. I cannot defend the order of preference but by saying that we have all some taste or other, of too ancient a date to admit of our remembering distinctly that it was an acquired one. I can call to mind the first play and the first exhibition that I was taken to; but I am not conscious of a time when china jars and saucers were introduced into my imagination.

I had no repugnance then (why should I now have?) to those little, lawless, azure-tinctured grotesques, that under the notion of men and women float about, uncircumscribed by any element, in that world before perspective—a china tea-cup.

I like to see my old friends—whom distance cannot diminish—figuring up in the air (so they appear to our optics), yet on *terra firma* still, for so we must in courtesy interpret that speck of deeper blue which the decorous artist, to prevent absurdity, had made to spring up beneath their sandals.

I love the men with women's faces, and the women, if possible, with still more womanish expressions.

Here is a young and courtly Mandarin, handing tea to a lady from a salver, two miles off. See how distance seems to set off respect! And here the same lady, or another, (for likeness is identity on teacups,) is stepping into a little fairy boat, moored on the hither side of this calm garden river, with a dainty mincing foot, which in a right angle of incidence (as angles go in our world) must infallibly land her in the midst of a flowery mead a furlong off on the other side of the same strange stream!

Farther on—if far or near can be predicated of their world—see horses, trees, pagodas, dancing the hays.

Here a cow and rabbit couchant and co-extensive; so objects show, seen through the lucid atmosphere of fine Cathay.

I was pointing out to my cousin last evening, over our Hyson, (which we are old-fashioned enough to drink unmixed still of an afternoon,) some of these *speciosa miracula* upon a set of extraordinary old blue china (a recent purchase) which we were now for the first time using; and could not help remarking how fa-

Essays

vourable circumstances had been to us of late years, that we could afford to please the eye sometimes with trifles of this sort, when a passing sentiment seemed to overshade the brows of my companion. I am quick at detecting these Summer clouds in Bridget.

"I wish the good old times would come again," she said, "when we were not quite so rich. I do not mean that I want to be poor; but there was a middle state," (so she was pleased to ramble on,) "in which I am sure we were a great deal happier. A purchase is but a purchase, now that you have money enough and to spare. Formerly it used to be a triumph. When we coveted a cheap luxury (and Oh, how much ado I had to get you to consent in those times!)—we were used to have a debate two or three days before, and to weigh the *for* and *against,* and think what we might spare it out of, and what saving we could hit upon, that should be an equivalent. A thing was worth buying then, when we felt the money that we paid for it.

"Do you remember the brown suit, which you made to hang upon you till all your friends cried shame upon you, it grew so thread-bare, and all because of that folio Beaumont and Fletcher, which you dragged home late at night from Barker's, in Covent Garden? Do you remember how we eyed it for weeks before we could make up our minds to the purchase, and had not come to a determination till

Charles Lamb

it was near ten o'clock of the Saturday night, when you set off from Islington, fearing you should be too late,—and when the old bookseller with some grumbling opened his shop, and by the twinkling taper (for he was setting bedwards) lighted out the relic from his dusty treasures,—and when you lugged it home, wishing it were twice as cumbersome,—and when you presented it to me,—and when we were exploring the perfectness of it (*collating* you called it),—and while I was repairing some of the loose leaves with paste, which your impatience would not suffer to be left till daybreak,—was there no pleasure in being a poor man? Or can those neat black clothes which you wear now, and are so careful to keep brushed, since we have become rich and finical, give you half the honest vanity with which you flaunted it about in that overworn suit—your old corbeau—for four or five weeks longer than you should have done, to pacify your conscience for the mighty sum of fifteen shillings—or sixteen was it? (a great affair we thought it then) which you had lavished on the old folio. Now you can afford to buy any book that pleases you, but I do not see that you ever bring me home any nice old purchases now.

"When you came home with twenty apologies for laying out a less number of shillings upon that print after Lionardo, which we christened the 'Lady Blanch;' when you looked at the purchase, and thought of the money—and looked

again at the picture, and thought of the money
—was there no pleasure in being a poor man?
Now you have nothing to do but to walk into
Colnaghi's, and buy a wilderness of Lionardos.
Yet do you?

"Then do you remember our pleasant walks
to Enfield, and Potter's Bar, and Waltham,
when we had a holyday, (holydays and all
other fun are gone now we are rich,) and the
little hand-basket in which I used to deposit
our day's fare of savoury cold lamb and salad
—and how you would pry about at noontide
for some decent house, where we might go in
and produce our store, only paying for the ale
that you must call for, and speculate upon the
looks of the landlady, and whether she was
likely to allow us a table-cloth,—and wish for
such another honest hostess as Izaak Walton
has described many a one on the pleasant banks
of the Lea, when he went a fishing; and sometimes they would prove obliging enough, and
sometimes they would look grudgingly upon
us; but we had cheerful looks still for one another, and would eat our plain food savourily,
scarcely grudging Piscator his Trout Hall.
Now, when we go out a day's pleasuring, which
is seldom moreover, we *ride* part of the way,
and go into a fine inn, and order the best of
dinners, never debating the expense, which,
after all, never has half the relish of those
chance country snaps, when we were at the

mercy of uncertain usage and a precarious welcome.

"You are too proud to see a play anywhere
now but in the pit. Do you remember where
it was we used to sit, when we saw the Battle
of Hexham, and the Surrender of Calais, and
Bannister and Mrs. Bland in the *Children in
the Wood*,—when we squeezed out our shillings a-piece to sit three or four times in a season in the one-shilling gallery, where you felt
all the time that you ought not to have brought
me, and more strongly I felt obligation to you
for having brought me,—and the pleasure was
the better for a little shame,—and when the
curtain drew up, what cared we for our place
in the house, or what mattered it where we were
sitting, when our thoughts were with Rosalind
in Arden, or with Viola at the Court of Illyria?
You used to say that the gallery was the best
place of all for enjoying a play socially; that
the relish of such exhibitions must be in proportion to the infrequency of going; that the
company we met there, not being in general
readers of plays, were obliged to attend the
more, and did attend, to what was going on on
the stage, because a word lost would have been
a chasm, which it was impossible for them to
fill up. With such reflections we consoled our
pride then; and I appeal to you whether, as a
woman, I met generally with less attention and
accommodation than I have done since in more
expensive situations in the house? Getting in

indeed, and crowding up those inconvenient staircases, was bad enough; but there was still a law of civility to woman recognised to quite as great an extent as we ever found in the other passages; and how a little difficulty overcome heightened the snug seat and the play, afterwards! Now we can only pay our money and walk in. You cannot see, you say, in the galleries now. I am sure we saw, and heard too, well enough then; but sight and all, I think, is gone with our poverty.

"There was pleasure in eating strawberries before they became quite common; in the first dish of pease while they were yet dear; to have them for a nice supper, a treat. What treat can we have now? If we were to treat ourselves now—that is, to have dainties a little above our means, it would be selfish and wicked. It is the very little more that we allow ourselves beyond what the actual poor can get at, that makes what I call a treat—when two people living together, as we have done, now and then indulge themselves in a cheap luxury, which both like; while each apologizes, and is willing to take both halves of the blame to his single share. I see no harm in people making much of themselves, in that sense of the word. It may give them a hint how to make much of others. But now, what I mean by the word—we never do make much of ourselves. None but the poor can do it. I do

Charles Lamb

not mean the veriest poor of all, but persons as we were, just above poverty.

"I know what you were going to say, that it is mighty pleasant at the end of the year to make all meet; and much ado we used to have every Thirty-first Night of December to account for our exceedings; many a long face did you make over your puzzled accounts, and in contriving to make it out how we had spent so much, or that we had not spent so much, or that it was impossible we should spend so much next year; and still we found our slender capital decreasing; but then,—betwixt ways, and projects, and compromises of one sort or another, and talk of curtailing this charge, and doing without that for the future, and the hope that youth brings, and laughing spirits, (in which you were never poor till now,) we pocketed up our loss, and in conclusion, with 'lusty brimmers,' (as you used to quote it out of *hearty cheerful Mr. Cotton,* as you called him,) we used to welcome in 'the coming guest.' Now we have no reckoning at all at the end of the Old Year,—no flattering promises about the New Year doing better for us."

Bridget is so sparing of her speech on most occasions, that when she gets into a rhetorical vein I am careful how I interrupt it. I could not help, however, smiling at the phantom of wealth which her dear imagination had conjured up out of a clear income of poor —— hundred pounds a year. "It is true we were happier when we were poorer, but we were also younger, my cousin. I am afraid we must put up with the excess, for if we were to shake the superflux into the sea we should not much mend ourselves. That we had much to struggle with, as we grew up together, we have reason to be most thankful. It strengthened and knit our compact closer. We could never have been what we have been to each other if we had always had the sufficiency which you now complain of. The resisting power—those natural dilations of the youthful spirit which circumstances cannot straiten—with us are long since passed away. Competence to age is supplementary youth; a sorry supplement indeed, but I fear the best that is to be had. We must ride where we formerly walked; live better and lie softer—and shall be wise to do so—than we had means to do in those good old days you speak of. Yet could those days return; could you and I once more walk our thirty miles a day; could Bannister and Mrs. Bland again be young, and you and I be young to see them; could the good old one-shilling gallery days return, (they are dreams, my cousin, now), but could you and I at this moment, instead of this quiet argument, by our well-carpeted fireside, sitting on this luxurious sofa, be once more struggling up those inconvenient staircases, pushed about, and squeezed, and elbowed by the poorest rabble of poor gallery scramblers; could I once more hear those anxious shrieks of yours, and the delicious *Thank God, we are safe,* which always followed when the topmost stair, conquered, let in the first light of the whole cheerful theatre down beneath us, I know not the fathom-line that ever touched a descent so deep as I would be willing to bury more wealth in than Crœsus had, or the great Jew R—— is supposed to have, to purchase it. And now do just look at that merry little Chinese waiter holding an umbrella, big enough for a bed-tester, over the head of that pretty insipid half Madona-ish chit of a lady in that very blue summer-house."

Letters

LETTERS

"* * * * * * Letters of dear Charles
Lamb, 'Saint Charles,' as Thackeray once
called him, while looking at one of his half-
mad letters and remembering his Devotion to
that quite mad Sister. I must say I think his
Letters infinitely better than his Essays; and
Patmore says his Conversation, when just
enough animated by Gin and Water, was better
than either: which I believe too. Procter said
he was far beyond the Coleridges, Wordsworths, Southeys, etc. And I am afraid I believe that also."

*Edward FitzGerald to C. E. Norton, June 10,
1876.*

TO COLERIDGE:

September 27, 1796.

My dearest Friend—White, or some of my
friends, or the public papers, by this time may
have informed you of the terrible calamities
that have fallen on our family. I will only

103

give you the outlines:—My poor dear, dearest sister, in a fit of insanity, has been the death of her own mother. I was at hand only time enough to snatch the knife out of her grasp. She is at present in a madhouse, from whence I fear she must be moved to an hospital. God has preserved to me my senses: I eat, and drink, and sleep, and have my judgment, I believe, very sound. My poor father was slightly wounded, and I am left to take care of him and my aunt. Mr. Norris, of the Bluecoat School, has been very very kind to us, and we have no other friend; but, thank God, I am very calm and composed, and able to do the best that remains to do. Write as religious a letter as possible, but no mention of what is gone and done with. With me "the former things are passed away," and I have something more to do than to feel.

God Almighty have us all in His keeping!

C. LAMB.

Mention nothing of poetry. I have destroyed every vestige of past vanities of that kind. Do as you please, but if you publish, publish mine (I give free leave) without name or initial, and never send me a book, I charge you.

Your own judgment will convince you not to take any notice of this yet to your dear wife. You look after your family; I have my reason and strength left to take care of mine. I charge you, don't think of coming to see me. Write.

I will not see you if you come. God Almighty love you and all of us! C. LAMB.

TO COLERIDGE:

October 3, 1796.

My dearest Friend—Your letter was an inestimable treasure to me. It will be a comfort to you, I know, to know that our prospects are somewhat brighter. My poor dear, dearest sister, the unhappy and unconscious instrument of the Almighty's judgments on our house, is restored to her senses,—to a dreadful sense and recollection of what has past, awful to her mind, and impressive (as it must be to the end of life), but tempered with religious resignation and the reasonings of a sound judgment, which, in this early stage, knows how to distinguish between a deed committed in a transient fit of frenzy and the terrible guilt of a mother's murder. I have seen her. I found her this morning, calm and serene; far, very far from an indecent forgetful serenity: she has a most affectionate and tender concern for what has happened. Indeed, from the beginning— frightful and hopeless as her disorder seemed— I had confidence enough in her strength of mind and religious principle, to look forward to a time when *even she* might recover tranquillity. God be praised, Coleridge! wonderful as it is to tell, I have never once been otherwise than collected and calm; even on the dreadful day, and in the midst of the terrible scene, I preserved a tranquillity which bystanders may have construed into indifference—a tranquillity not of despair. Is it folly or sin in me to say that it was a religious principle that *most* supported me? I allow much to other favourable circumstances. I felt that I had something else to do than to regret. On that first evening my aunt was lying insensible—to all appearance like one dying; my father, with his poor forehead plaistered over from a wound he had received from a daughter, dearly loved by him, and who loved him no less dearly; my mother a dead and murdered corpse in the next room; yet was I wonderfully supported. I closed not my eyes in sleep that night, but lay without terrors and without despair. I have lost no sleep since. I had been long used not to rest in things of sense,—had endeavoured after a comprehension of mind, unsatisfied with the "ignorant present time;" and *this* kept me up. I had the whole weight of the family thrown on me; for my brother, little disposed (I speak not without tenderness for him) at any time to take care of old age and infirmities, had now, with his bad leg, an exemption from such duties, and I was now left alone. One little incident may serve to make you understand my way of managing my mind: Within a day or two after the fatal one, we dressed for dinner a tongue, which we had had salted for some weeks in the house. As I sat down, a feeling like remorse struck me: this tongue poor Mary got for me; and can I partake of it now, when she is far away? A thought occurred and relieved me:—if I give into this way of feeling, there is not a chair, a room, an object in our rooms, that will not awaken the keenest griefs. I must rise above such weaknesses. I hope this was not want of true feeling. I did not let this carry me, though, too far. On the very second day (I date from the day of horrors), as is usual in such cases, there were a matter of twenty people, I do think, supping in our room: they prevailed on me to eat *with them* (for to eat I never refused). They were all making merry in the room! Some had come from friendship, some from busy curiosity, and some from interest. I was going to partake with them, when my recollection came that my poor dead mother was lying in the next room—the very next room;—a mother who, through life, wished nothing but her children's welfare. Indignation, the rage of grief, something like remorse, rushed upon my mind. In an agony of emotion I found my way mechanically to the adjoining room, and fell on my knees by the side of her coffin, asking forgiveness of Heaven, and sometimes of her, for forgetting her so soon. Tranquillity returned, and it was the only violent emotion that mastered me. I think it did me good.

I mention these things because I hate concealment, and love to give a faithful journal of what passes within me. Our friends have been very good. Sam Le Grice, who was then in town, was with me the first three or four days, and was as a brother to me; gave up every hour of his time, to the very hurting of his health and spirits, in constant attendance and humouring my poor father; talked with him, read to him, played at cribbage with him (for so short is the old man's recollection, that he was playing at cards, as though nothing had happened, while the coroner's inquest was sitting over the way!) Samuel wept tenderly when he went away, for his mother wrote him a very severe letter on his loitering so long in town, and he was forced to go. Mr. Norris, of Christ's Hospital, has been as a father to me—Mrs. Norris as a mother; though we had few claims on them. A gentleman, brother to my godmother, from whom we never had right or reason to expect any such assistance, sent my father twenty pounds; and to crown all these God's blessings to our family at such a time, an old lady, a cousin of my father and aunt's, a gentlewoman of fortune, is to take my aunt and make her comfortable for the short remainder of her days. My aunt is recovered, and as well as ever, and highly pleased at thoughts of going—and has generously given up the interest of her little money (which was formerly paid my father for her board) wholely and solely to my sister's use. Reckoning this, we have, Daddy and I, for our two selves and

an old maid-servant to look after him, when
I am out, which will be necessary, £170 (or
£180 rather) a-year, out of which we can spare
£50 or £60 at least for Mary while she stays
at Islington, where she must and shall stay
during her father's life, for his and her comfort. I know John will make speeches about it,
but she shall not go into an hospital. The good
lady of the madhouse, and her daughter, an ele-
gant, sweet-behaved young lady, love her, and
are taken with her amazingly; and I know from
her own mouth she loves them, and longs to be
with them as much. Poor thing, they say she
was but the other morning saying she knew she
must go to Bethlem for life; that one of her
brothers would have it so, but the other would
wish it not, but be obliged to go with the
stream; that she had often as she passed Bethlem thought it likely, "here it may be my fate
to end my days," conscious of a certain flight-
iness in her poor head oftentimes, and mind-
ful of more than one severe illness of that
nature before. A legacy of £100, which my
father will have at Christmas, and this £20 I
mentioned before, with what is in the house,
will much more than set us clear. If my father,
an old servant-maid, and I, can't live, and live
comfortably, on £130 or £120 a-year, we ought
to burn by slow fires; and I almost would, that
Mary might not go into an hospital. Let me
not leave one unfavourable impression on your
mind respecting my brother. Since this has

happened, he has been very kind and brotherly; but I fear for his mind: he has taken his ease in the world, and is not fit himself to struggle with difficulties, nor has much accustomed himself to throw himself into their way; and I know his language is already, "Charles, you must take care of yourself; you must not abridge yourself of a single pleasure you have been used to," etc., etc., and in that style of talking. But you, a Necessarian, can respect a difference of mind, and love what *is amiable* in a character not perfect. He has been very good; but I fear for his mind. Thank God, I can unconnect myself with him, and shall manage all my father's moneys in future myself, if I take charge of Daddy, which poor John has not even hinted a wish, at any future time even, to share with me. The lady at this madhouse assures me that I may dismiss immediately both doctor and apothecary, retaining occasionally a composing draught or so for a while; and there is a less expensive establishment in her house, where she will only not have a room and nurse to herself, for £50 or guineas a-year—the outside would be £60. You know, by economy, how much more even I shall be able to spare for her comforts. She will I fancy, if she stays, make one of the family, rather than of the patients; and the old and young ladies I like exceedingly, and she loves dearly; and they, as the saying is, take to her very extraordinarily, if it is extraordinary that people who see my sister should love her. Of all the people I ever saw in the world, my poor sister was most and thoroughly devoid of the least tincture of selfishness. I will enlarge upon her qualities, poor dear, dearest soul, in a future letter, for my own comfort, for I understand her thoroughly; and, if I mistake not, in the most trying situation that a human being can be found in, she will be found—(I speak not with sufficient humility, I fear), but humanly and foolishly speaking, she will be found, I trust, uniformly great and amiable. God keep her in her present mind!—to whom be thanks and praise for all His dispensations to mankind.

C. LAMB.

These mentioned good fortunes and change of prospects had almost brought my mind over to the extreme, the very opposite to despair. I was in danger of making myself too happy. Your letter brought me back to a view of things which I had entertained from the beginning. I hope (for Mary I can answer)—but I hope that *I* shall through life never have less recollection nor a fainter impression of what has happened than I have now. 'Tis not a light thing, nor meant by the Almighty to be received lightly. I must be serious, circumspect, and deeply religious through life; and by such means may *both* of us escape madness in future, if it so please the Almighty.

Send me word how it fares with Sara. I repeat it, your letter was, and will be, an inestimable treasure to me. You have a view of what my situation demands of me, like my own view, and I trust a just one.

Coleridge, continue to write; but do not forever offend me by talking of sending me cash. Sincerely, and on my soul, we do not want it. God love you both!

I will write again very soon. Do you write directly.

TO MANNING*

November 28, 1800.

Dear Manning—I have received a very kind invitation from Lloyd and Sophia, to go and spend a month with them at the Lakes. Now it fortunately happens (which is so seldom the case) that I have spare cash by me, enough to answer the expenses of so long a journey; and I am determined to get away from the office by some means. The purpose of this letter is to request of you (my dear friend), that you will not take it unkind if I decline my proposed visit to Cambridge *for the present*. Perhaps I shall be able to take Cambridge *in my way*, going or coming. I need not describe to you the ex-

---

*Thomas Manning (1772-1840), a brilliant mathematician, tutor at Caius College, Cambridge, where Lamb first met him, and afterwards for many years an explorer in China.

ULLSWATER IN CUMBERLAND

pectations which such an one as myself, pent up all my life in a dirty city, have formed of a tour to the Lakes. Consider Grasmere! Ambleside! Wordsworth! Coleridge! I hope you will. Hills, woods, lakes, and mountains, to the devil. I will eat snipes with thee, Thomas Manning. Only confess, confess, a *bite*.

P. S.—I think you named the 16th; but was it not modest of Lloyd to send such an invitation! It shows his knowledge of *money* and *time*. I should be loth to think he meant

> "Ironic satire sidelong sklented
> On my poor pursie."—BURNS.

For my part, with reference to my friends northward, I must confess that I am not romance-bit about *Nature*. The earth, and sea, and sky (when all is said), is but as a house to dwell in. If the inmates be courteous, and good liquors flow like the conduits at an old coronation, if they can talk sensibly, and feel properly, I have no need to stand staring upon the gilded looking-glass (that strained my friend's purse-strings in the purchase) nor his five-shilling print, over the mantlepiece of old Nabbs the carrier (which only betrays his false taste). Just as important to me (in a sense) is all the furniture of my world; eye-pampering, but satisfies no heart. Streets, streets, streets, markets, theatres, churches, Covent Gardens, shops sparkling with pretty faces of industrious milliners, neat sempstresses, ladies cheapening, gentlemen behind counters, lying, authors in the street with spectacles, George Dyers (you may know them by their gait), lamps lit at night, pastrycooks' and silver-smiths' shops, beautiful Quakers of Pentonville, noise of coaches, drowsy cry of mechanic watchmen at night, with bucks reeling home drunk; if you happen to wake at midnight, cries of "Fire!" and "Stop thief!"; inns of court, with their learned air, and halls, and butteries, just like Cambridge colleges; old book-stalls, "Jeremy Taylors," "Burtons on Melancholy," and "Religio Medicis," on every stall. These are thy pleasures, O London! with thy many sins. O City, abounding in w . . ., for these may Keswick and her giant brood go hang!

C. L.

TO WORDSWORTH

January 30, 1801.

I ought before this to have replied to your very kind invitation into Cumberland. With you and your sister I could gang anywhere; but I am afraid whether I shall ever be able to af-ford so desperate a journey. Separate from the pleasure of your company, I don't much care if I never see a mountain in my life. I have passed all my days in London, until I have formed as many and intense local attach-ments as any of you mountaineers can have done with dead Nature. The lighted shops of the Strand and Fleet Street; the innumerable trades, tradesmen, and customers, coaches, wagons, playhouses; all the bustle and wickedness round about Covent Garden; the very women of the Town; the watchmen, drunken scenes, rattles; life awake, if you awake, at all hours of the night; the impossibility of being dull in Fleet Street; the crowds, the very dirt and mud, the sun shining upon houses and pavements, the print-shops, the old book-stalls, parsons cheapening books, coffee-houses, steams of soups from kitchens, the pantomimes —London itself a pantomime and a masquerade —all these things work themselves into my mind, and feed me, without a power of satiating me. The wonder of these sights impels me into night-walks about her crowded streets, and I often shed tears in the motley Strand from fulness of joy at so much life. All these emotions must be strange to you; so are your rural emotions to me. But consider, what must I have been doing all my life, not to have lent great portions of my heart with usury to such scenes?

My attachments are all local, purely local. I have no passion (or have had none since I was in love, and then it was the spurious engendering of poetry and books) for groves and valleys. The rooms where I was born, the furniture which has been before my eyes all my life, the book-case which has followed me about

Charles Lamb

like a faithful dog, (only exceeding him in knowledge), wherever I have moved, old chairs, old tables, streets, squares, where I have sunned myself, my old school,—these are my mistresses. Have I not enough, without your mountains? I do not envy you. I should pity you, did I not know that the mind will make friends of anything. Your sun, and moon, and skies, and hills, and lakes, affect me no more, or scarcely come to me in more vener ble characters, than as a gilded room with tapestry and tapers, where I might live with handsome visible objects. I consider the clouds above me but as a roof beautifully painted, but unable to satisfy the mind: and at last, like the pictures of the apartment of a connoisseur, unable to afford him any longer a pleasure. So fading upon me, from disuse, have been the beauties of Nature, as they have been confinedly called; so ever fresh, and green, and warm are all the inventions of men, and assemblies of men in this great city. I should certainly have laughed with dear Joanna.

Give my kindest love, and my sister's, to D. and yourself; and a kiss from me to little Barbara Lewthwaite. Thank you for liking my play.

C. L.

Letters

TO THOMAS MANNING

London, September 24, 1802.

My dear Manning—Since the date of my last
letter I have been a traveller. A strong desire
seized me of visiting remote regions. My first
impulse was to go and see Paris. It was a
trivial objection to my aspiring mind, that I
did not understand a word of the language,
since I certainly intend some time in my life
to see Paris, and equally certainly intend never
to learn the language; therefore that could be
no objection. However, I am very glad I did
not go, because you had left Paris (I see) before I could have set out. I believe, Stoddart
promising to go with me another year, prevented that plan. My next scheme (for to my
restless, ambitious mind London was become a
bed of thorns) was to visit the far-famed peak
in Derbyshire, where the Devil sits, they say,
without breeches. *This* my purer mind rejected
as indelicate. And my final resolve was, a
tour to the Lakes. I set out with Mary to
Keswick, without giving Coleridge any notice,
for my time, being precious, did not admit of
it. He received us with all the hospitality in
the world, and gave up his time to show us all
the wonders of the country. He dwells upon a
small hill by the side of Keswick, in a comfortable house, quite enveloped on all sides by
a net of mountains: great floundering bears

and monsters they seemed, all couchant and
asleep. We got in in the evening, travelling in
a post-chaise from Penrith, in the midst of a
gorgeous sunshine, which transmuted all the
mountains into colours, purple, etc. etc. We
thought we had got into fairyland. But that
went off (as it never came again; while we
stayed we had no more fine sunsets), and we
entered Coleridge's comfortable study just in
the dusk, when the mountains were all dark
with clouds upon their heads. Such an impression I never received from objects of sight before, nor do I suppose I can ever again. Glorious creatures, fine old fellows, Skiddaw, etc. I
never shall forget ye, how ye lay about that
night, like an intrenchment; gone to bed, as it
seemed for the night, but promising that ye
were to be seen in the morning. Coleridge had
got a blazing fire in his study; which is a large
antique, ill-shaped room, with an old-fashioned organ, never played upon, big enough for
a church, shelves of scattered folios, an Æolian
harp, and an old sofa, half bed, etc. And all
looking out upon the last fading view of Skid
daw, and his broad-breasted brethren: what a
night! Here we stayed three full weeks, in
which time I visited Wordsworth's cottage,
where we stayed a day or two with the Clarksons (good people, and most hospitable, at
whose house we tarried one day and night),
and saw Lloyd. The Wordsworths were gone
to Calais. They have since been in London,

and past much time with us: he is now gone
into Yorkshire to be married. So we have seen
Keswick, Grasmere, Ambleside, Ulswater
(where the Clarksons live), and a place at the
other end of Ulswater; I forget the name; to
which we travelled on a very sultry day, over
the middle of Helvellyn. We have clambered
up to the top of Skiddaw, and I have waded up
the bed of Lodore. In fine, I have satisfied myself that there is such a thing as that which
tourists call *romantic,* which I very much suspected before: they make such a spluttering
about it, and toss their splendid epithets around
them, till they give as dim a light as at four
o'clock next morning the lamps do after an illumination. Mary was excessively tired when
she got about half-way up Skiddaw, but we
came to a cold rill (than which nothing can be
imagined more cold, running over cold stones),
and with the reinforcement of a draught of
cold water she surmounted it most manfully.
Oh, its fine black head, and the bleak air atop
of it, with a prospect of mountains all about
and about, making you giddy; and then Scot-
land afar off, and the border countries so famous in song and ballad! It was a day that
will stand out like a mountain, I am sure, in
my life. But I am returned (I have now been
come home near three weeks; I was a month
out), and you cannot conceive the degradation
I felt at first, from being accustomed to wander
free as air among mountains, and bathe in

rivers without being controlled by any one, to come home and *work*. I felt very *little*. I had been dreaming I was a very great man. But that is going off, and I find I shall conform in time to that state of life to which it has pleased God to call me. Besides, after all, Fleet Street and the Strand are better places to live in for good and all than amidst Skiddaw. Still I turn back to those great places where I wandered about, participating in their greatness. After all, I could not *live* in Skiddaw. I could spend a year, two, three years among them, but I must have a prospect of seeing Fleet Street at the end of that time, or I should mope and pine away, I know. Still, Skiddaw is a fine creature. My habits are changing, I think, *i. e.* from drunk to sober. Whether I shall be happier or not remains to be proved. I shall certainly be more happy in a morning; but whether I shall not sacrifice the fat, and the marrow, and the kidneys, *i. e.* the night, glorious care-drowning night, that heals all our wrongs, pours wine into our mortifications, changes the scene from indifferent and flat to bright and brilliant! O Manning, if I should have formed a diabolical resolution, by the time you come to England, of not admitting any spirituous liquors into my house, will you be my guest on such shameworthy terms? Is life, with such limitations, worth trying? The truth is, that my liquors bring a nest of friendly harpies about my house, who consume me. This is a pitiful tale to be read at St. Gothard, but it is just now nearest my heart. Fenwick is a ruined man. He is hiding himself from his creditors, and has sent his wife and children into the country. Fell, my other drunken companion (that has been: *nam hic cæstus artemque repono*), is turned editor of a Naval Chronicle. Godwin continues a steady friend, though the same facility does not remain of visiting him often. That . . . has detached Marshall from his house; Marshall, the man who went to sleep when the "Ancient Mariner" was reading; the old, steady, unalterable friend of the Professor. Holcroft is not yet come to town. I expect to see him, and will deliver your message. Things come crowding in to say, and no room for 'em. Some things are too little to be told,—*i. e.* to have a preference; some are too big and circumstantial. Thanks for yours, which was most delicious. Would I had been with you, benighted, etc.! I fear my head is turned with wandering. I shall never be the same acquiescent being. Farewell. Write again quickly, for I shall not like to hazard a letter, not knowing where the fates have carried you. Farewell, my dear fellow.

C. LAMB.

Charles Lamb

To Miss HUTCHINSON*

Thursday, October 19, 1815.

Dear Miss H.—I am forced to be the replier to your letter, for Mary has been ill, and gone from home these five weeks yesterday. She has left me very lonely and very miserable. I stroll about, but there is no rest but at one's own fireside, and there is no rest for me there now. I look forward to the worse half being past, and keep up as well as I can. She has begun to show some favourable symptoms. The return of her disorder has been frightfully soon this time, with scarce a six months' interval. I am almost afraid my worry of spirits about the E. I. House was partly the cause of her illness, but one always imputes it to the cause next at hand; more probably it comes from some cause we have no control over or conjecture of. It cuts sad great slices out of the time, the little time, we shall have to live together. I don't know but the recurrence of these illnesses might help me to sustain her death better than if we had had no partial separations. But I won't talk of death. I will imagine us immortal, or forget that we are otherwise. By God's blessing, in a few weeks we may be making our meal together, or sitting in the front row of the Pit at Drury Lane, or taking our evening walk past

*Miss Hutchinson was a sister of Wordsworth's wife.

the theatres, to look at the outside of them, at least, if not to be tempted in. Then we forget we are assailable; we are strong for the time as rocks;—"the wind is tempered to the shorn Lambs." Poor C. Lloyd, and poor Priscilla! I feel I hardly feel enough for him; my own calamities press about me, and involve me in a thick integument not to be reached at by other folks' misfortunes. But I feel all I can—all the kindness I can towards you all—God bless you! I hear nothing from Coleridge.

Yours truly,   C. LAMB.

To J. TAYLOR.*

July 30, 1821.

Dear Sir—You will do me injustice if you do not convey to the writer of the beautiful lines, which I now return you, my sense of the extreme kindness which dictated them. Poor Elia (call him *Ellia*) does not pretend to so very clear revelations of a future state of being as Olen seems gifted with. He stumbles about dark mountains at best; but he knows at least how to be thankful for this life, and is too thankful indeed for certain relationships lent him here, not to tremble for a possible resumption of the gift. He is too apt to express himself lightly, and cannot be sorry for the pres-

---

*Lamb's publisher. This letter explains the origin of the nom-de-plume "Elia."

ent occasion, as it has called forth a reproof **so** Christian-like. His *animus* at least (whatever become of it in the female termination) hath always been *cum Christianis.*

Pray make my gratefullest respects to the Poet (do I flatter myself when I hope it may be M——y?) and say how happy I should feel myself in an acquaintance with him. I will just mention that in the middle of the second column, where I have affixed a cross, the line

"One in a skeleton's ribb'd hollow cooped,"

is undoubtedly wrong. Should it not be—

"A skeleton's rib or ribs?"

or,

"In a skeleton ribb'd, hollow-coop'd?"

I perfectly remember the plate in Quarles. In the first page esoteric is pronounced esóteric. It should be (if that is the word) esotéric. The false accent may be corrected by omitting the word *old.* Pray, for certain reasons, give me to the 18th *at farthest extremity* for my next.

Poor ELIA, the real (for I am but a counterfeit), is dead. The fact is, a person of that name, an Italian, was a fellow-clerk of mine at the South Sea House, thirty (not forty) years ago, when the characters I described there existed, but had left it like myself many years; and I having a brother now there, and doubting how he might relish certain descriptions in it, I clapt down the name of Elia to it, which passed off pretty well, for Elia himself added the function of an author to that of a scrivener, like myself.

I went the other day (not having seen him for a year) to laugh over with him at my usurpation of his name, and found him, alas! no more than a name, for he died of consumption eleven months ago, and I knew not of it.

So the name has fairly devolved to me, I think; and 'tis all he has left me.

Dear sir, yours truly,   C. LAMB.

Messrs. Taylor & Hessey, Fleet Street,
        for J. Taylor, Esq.

To J. TAYLOR.

December 7, 1822.

DEAR SIR—I should like the enclosed Dedication to be printed, unless you dislike it. I like it. It is in the olden style. But if you object to it, put forth the book as it is; only pray don't let the printer mistake the word *curt* for *curst*.
                                    C. L.

DEDICATION

TO THE FRIENDLY AND JUDICIOUS READER,

who will take these Papers, as they were meant; not understanding everything perversely in its absolute and literal sense, but giving fair construction, as to an after-dinner con-

Charles Lamb

versation; allowing for the rashness and necessary incompleteness of first thoughts; and not
remembering, for the purpose of an after taunt,
words spoken peradventure after the fourth
glass, the Author wishes (what he would will
for himself) plenty of good friends to stand by
him, good books to solace him, prosperous
events to all his honest undertakings, and a
candid interpretation to his most hasty words
and actions. The other sort (and he hopes
many of them will purchase his book too)
he greets with the curt invitation of Timon,
"Uncover, dogs, and lap:" or he dismisses
them with the confident security of the philos-
opher,—"you beat but on the case of Elia." On
better consideration, pray omit that Dedication.
The Essays want no Preface: they are *all
Preface*. A Preface is nothing but a talk with
the reader; and they do nothing else. Pray
omit it.

There will be a sort of Preface in the next
Magazine, which may act as an advertisement,
but not proper for the volume.

Let ELIA come forth bare as he was born.

C. L.

Messrs. Taylor and Hessey,
   Booksellers, Fleet Street.
No Preface.

To BERNARD BARTON.*

January 9, 1823.

"Throw yourself on the world without any rational plan of support, beyond what the chance employ of booksellers would afford you!!!"

Throw yourself rather, my dear sir, from the steep Tarpeian rock, slap-dash headlong upon iron spikes. If you had but five consolatory minutes between the desk and the bed make much of them, and live a century in them, rather than turn slave to the booksellers. They are Turks and Tartars when they have poor authors at their beck. Hitherto you have been at arm's length from them. Come not within their grasp. I have known many authors for bread, some repining, others envying the blessed security of a counting-house, all agreeing they would rather have been tailors, weavers,—what not, rather than the things they were. I have known some starved, some to go mad, one dear friend literally dying in a workhouse. You know not what a rapacious, dishonest set these booksellers are. Ask even Southey, who (a single case almost) has made a fortune by book drudgery, what he

*The "Quaker poet," a bank clerk in Wood-bridge, Suffolk. His daughter married Edward Fitzgerald, who published in 1849 a volume of selections from Barton's poetry.

has found them. Oh, you know not (may you never know!) the miseries of subsisting by authorship. 'Tis a pretty appendage to a situation like yours or mine; but a slavery, worse than all slavery, to be a bookseller's dependent, to drudge your brains for pots of ale and breasts of mutton, to change your free thoughts and voluntary numbers for ungracious task-work. Those fellows hate *us*. The reason I take to be, that contrary to other trades, in which the master gets all the credit (a jeweller or silversmith for instance), and the journeyman, who really does the fine work, is in the background,—in *our* work the world gives all the credit to us, whom *they* consider as *their* journeymen, and therefore do they hate us, and cheat us, and oppress us, and would wring the blood of us out, to put another sixpence in their mechanic pouches! I contend that a bookseller has a *relative honesty* towards authors, not like his honesty to the rest of the world. B., who first engaged me as "Elia," has not paid me up yet (nor any of us without repeated mortifying appeals), yet how the knave fawned when I was of service to him! Yet I dare say the fellow is punctual in settling his milk-score, etc.

Keep to your bank, and the bank will keep you. Trust not to the public; you may hang, starve, drown yourself, for anything that worthy *personage* cares. I bless every star that Providence, not seeing good to make me independent, has seen it next good to settle me upon the stable foundation of Leadenhall. Sit down, good B. B., in the banking-office. What! is there not from six to eleven *p.m.* six days in the week, and is there not all Sunday? Fie, what a superfluity of man's time, if you could think so!—enough for relaxation, mirth, converse, poetry, good thoughts, quiet thoughts. Oh the corroding, torturing, tormenting thoughts, that disturb the brain of the unlucky wight who must draw upon it for daily sustenance! Henceforth I retract all my fond complaints of mercantile employment; look upon them as lovers' quarrels. I was but half in earnest. Welcome dead timber of a desk, that makes me live. A little grumbling is a wholesome medicine for the spleen; but in my inner heart do I approve and embrace this our close but unharassing way of life. I am quite serious. If you can send me Fox, I will not keep it *six weeks,* and will return it, with warm thanks to yourself and friend, without blot or dog's ear. You will much oblige me by this kindness.

Yours truly,   C. LAMB.

TO WILLIAM WORDSWORTH

Colebrook Cottage, April 6, 1825.

Dear Wordsworth—I have been several times meditating a letter to you concerning the good thing which has befallen me, but the thought of poor Monkhouse came across me. He was one that I had exulted in the prospect of congratulating me. He and you were to have been the first participators, for indeed it has been ten weeks since the first motion of it. Here am I then, after thirty-three years' slavery, sitting in my own room at eleven o'clock this finest of all April mornings, a freed man, with £441 a year for the remainder of my life, live I as long as John Dennis, who outlived his annuity and starved at ninety; £441, *i. e.* £450, with a deduction of £9 for a provision secured to my sister, she being survivor, the pension guaranteed by Act Georgii Tertii, etc.

I came home FOR EVER on Tuesday in last week. The incomprehensibleness of my condition overwhelmed me. It was like passing from life into eternity. Every year to be as long as three, *i. e.* to have three times as much real time (time that is my own) in it! I wandered about thinking I was happy, but feeling I was not. But that tumultuousness is passing off, and I begin to understand the nature of the gift. Holydays, even the annual month, were always uneasy joys; their conscious fugitiveness; the craving after making the most of them. Now, when all is holyday, there are no holydays. I can sit at home, in rain or shine, without a restless impulse for walkings. I am daily steadying, and shall soon find it as natural to me to be my own master, as it has been irksome to have had a master. Mary wakes every morning with an obscure feeling that some good has happened to us.

Leigh Hunt and Montgomery, after their releasements, describe the shock of their emancipation much as I feel mine. But it hurt their frames. I eat, drink, and sleep as sound as ever. I lay no anxious schemes for going hither and thither, but take things as they occur. Yesterday I excursioned twenty miles; to-day I write a few letters. Pleasuring was for fugitive play-days; mine are fugitive only in the sense that life is fugitive. Freedom and life co-existent!

At the foot of such a call upon you for gratulation, I am ashamed to advert to that melancholy event. Monkhouse was a character I learned to love slowly, but it grew upon me, yearly, monthly, daily. What a chasm has it made in our pleasant parties! His noble friendly face was always coming before me, till this hurrying event in my life came, and for the time has absorbed all interest; in fact it has shaken me a little. My old desk companions, with whom I have had such merry hours, seem to reproach me for removing my lot from among them. They were pleasant creatures; but to the anxieties of business, and a weight of possible worse ever impending, I was not equal. Tuthill and Gillman gave me my certificates. I laughed at the friendly lie implied in them; but my sister shook her head, and said it was all true. Indeed, this last Winter I was jaded out: Winters were always worse than other parts of the year, because the spirits are worse, and I had no daylight. In Summer I had day-light evenings. The relief was hinted to me from a superior Power, when I, poor slave, had not a hope but that I must wait another seven years with Jacob: and lo! the Rachel which I coveted is brought to me!

Have you read the noble dedication of Irving's "Missionary Orations" to S. T. C.? Who shall call this man a quack hereafter? What the Kirk will think of it neither I nor Irving care. When somebody suggested to him that it would not be likely to do him good, videlicet, among his own people, "That is a reason for doing it," was his noble answer. That Irving thinks he has profited mainly by S. T. C., I have no doubt. The very style of the Dedication shows it.

Communicate my news to Southey, and beg his pardon for my being so long acknowledging his kind present of the "Church," which circumstances, having no reference to himself, prevented at the time. Assure him of my deep respect and friendliest feelings.

Divide the same, or rather each take the whole to you—I mean you and all yours. To Miss Hutchinson I must write separate.

Farewell! and end at last, long selfish letter.

C. LAMB.

TO BERNARD BARTON

Enfield Chase Side, Saturday,
25th of July, A. D. 1829, 11 A. M.

There!—a fuller, plumper, juicier date never
dropt from Idumean palm. Am I in the *date-*
ive case now? If not, a fig for dates, which
is more than a date is worth. I never stood
much affected to these limitary specialties; least
of all, since the date of my superannuation.

"What have I with time to do?
Slaves of desks, 'twas meant for you."

Dear B. B.—Your handwriting has conveyed
much pleasure to me in report of Lucy's restoration. Would I could send you as good
news of my poor Lucy. But some wearisome
weeks I must remain lonely yet. I have had
the loneliest time, near ten weeks, broken by a
short apparition of Emma for her holidays,
whose departure only deepened the returning
solitude, and by ten days I have past in town.
But town, with all my native hankering after
it, is not what it was. The streets, the shops
are left; but all old friends are gone! And in
London I was frightfully convinced of this as
I passed houses and places, empty caskets now.
I have ceased to care almost about anybody.
The bodies I cared for are in graves, or dis-
persed. My old clubs, that lived so long and
flourished so steadily, are crumbled away.

When I took leave of our adopted young friend at Charing Cross, 'twas heavy unfeeling rain, and I had nowhere to go. Home have I none, and not a sympathising house to turn to in the great city. Never did the waters of heaven pour down on a forlorner head. Yet I tried ten days at a sort of friend's house, but it was large and straggling,—one of the individuals of my old long knot of friends, card-players, pleasant companions, that have tumbled to pieces, into dust and other things; and I got home on Thursday, convinced that I was better to get home to my hole at Enfield, and hide like a sick cat in my corner. Less than a month I hope will bring home Mary. She is at Fulham, looking better in her health than ever, but sadly rambling, and scarce showing any pleasure in seeing me, or curiosity when I should come again. But the old feelings will come back again, and we shall drown old sorrows over a game of picquet again. But 'tis a tedious cut out of a life of sixty-four, to lose twelve or thirteen weeks every year or two. And to make me more alone, our ill-tempered maid is gone, who, with all her airs, was yet a home-piece of furniture, a record of better days. The young thing that has succeeded her is good and attentive, but she is nothing. And I have no one here to talk over old matters with. Scolding and quarrelling have something of familiarity, and a community of interest; they imply acquaintance; they are of resentment, which is of the family of dearness.

I can neither scold nor quarrel at this insignificant implement of household services: she is less than a cat, and just better than a deal dresser. What I can do, and do overdo, is to walk; but deadly long are the days, these Summer all-day days, with but a half-hour's candle-light, and no fire-light. I do not write, tell your kind inquisitive Eliza, and can hardly read. In the ensuing *Blackwood* will be an old dejected farce of mine, which may be new to you, if you see that same medley. What things are all the magazines now! I contrive studiously not to see them. The popular *New Monthly* is perfect trash. Poor Hessey, I suppose you see, has failed; Hunt and Clarke too. Your "Vulgar Truths" will be a good name; and I think your prose must please—me at least. But 'tis useless to write poetry with no purchasers. 'Tis cold work authorship, without something to puff one into fashion. Could you not write something on Quakerism, for Quakers to read, but nominally addressed to Non-Quakers, explaining your dogmas—waiting on the Spirit—by the analogy of human calmness and patient waiting on the judgment? I scarcely know what I mean, but to make Non-Quakers reconciled to your doctrines, by showing something like them in mere human operations; but I hardly understand myself; so let it pass for nothing. I pity you for overwork; but I assure you, no work is worse. The mind preys on itself, the most unwholesome food. I bragged formerly that I could not have too much time. I have a surfeit. With few years to come, the days are wearisome. But weariness is not eternal. Something will shine out to take the load off that flags me, which is at present intolerable. I have killed an hour or two in this poor scrawl. I am a sanguinary murderer of time, and would kill him inchmeal just now. But the snake is vital. Well: I shall write merrier anon. 'Tis the present copy of my countenance I send, and to complain is a little to alleviate. May you enjoy yourself as far as the wicked wood will let you, and think that you are not quite alone as I am! Health to Lucia, and to Anna, and kind remembrances. Your forlorn, C. L.

TO WILLIAM WORDSWORTH

January 22, 1830.

And is it a year since we parted from you at the steps of Edmonton stage? There are not now the years that there used to be. The tale of the dwindled age of men, reported of successional mankind, is true of the same man only. We do not live a year in a year now. 'Tis a *punctum stans.* The seasons pass us with indifference. Spring cheers not, nor Winter heightens our gloom; Autumn hath foregone its moralities,—they are "hey-pass re-

pass," as in a show-box. Yet, as far as last
year occurs back,—for they scarce show a reflex now, they make no memory as heretofore,
—'twas sufficiently gloomy. Let the sullen
nothing pass. Suffice it that after sad spirits,
prolonged through many of its months, as it
called them, we have cast our skins; have taken
a farewell of the pompous, troublesome trifle,
called housekeeping, and are settled down into
poor boarders and lodgers at next door with an
old couple, the Baucis and Baucida of dull Enfield. Here we have nothing to do with our
victuals but to eat them; with the garden but
to see it grow; with the tax-gatherer but to
hear him knock; with the maid but to hear her
scolded. Scot and lot, butcher, baker, are
things unknown to us, save as spectators of the
pageant. We are fed we know not how;
quietists—confiding ravens. We have *otium
pro dignitate,* a respectable insignificance. Yet
in the self-condemned obliviousness, in the
stagnation, some molesting yearnings of life,
not quite killed, rise, prompting me that there
was a London, and that I was of that old
Jerusalem. In dreams I am in Fleet Market,
but I wake and cry to sleep again. I die hard,
a stubborn Eloisa in this detestable Paraclete.
What have I gained by health? Intolerable
dulness. What by early hours and moderate
meals? A total blank. O never let the lying
poets be believed, who 'tice men from the
cheerful haunts of streets, or think they mean

it not of a country village. In the ruins of
Palmyra I could gird myself up to solitude, or
muse to the snorings of the Seven Sleepers; but
to have a little teazing image of a town about
one; country folks that do not look like country folks; shops two yards square, half-a-dozen
apples, and two penn'orth of overlooked gin-
ger-bread for the lofty fruiterers of Oxford
Street; and, for the immortal book and print
stalls a circulating library that stands still,
where the show-picture is a last year's Valen-
tine, and whither the fame of the last ten
Scotch novels has not yet travelled,—(marry,
they just begin to be conscious of the *Red-
gauntlet:*)—to have a new plastered flat
church, and to be wishing that it was but a
cathedral! The very blackguards here are de-
generate; the topping gentry stock-brokers; the
passengers too many to insure your quiet, or
let you go about whistling or gaping, too few
to be the fine indifferent pageants of Fleet
Street. Confiding, room-keeping, thickest Winter, is yet more bearable here than the gaudy
months. Among one's books at one's fire by
candle, one is soothed into an oblivion that one
is not in the country; but with the light the
green fields return, till I gaze, and in a calen-
ture can plunge myself into St. Giles's. O let
no native Londoner imagine that health, and
rest, and innocent occupation, interchange of
converse sweet, and recreative study, can make
the country anything better than altogether

odious and detestable! A garden was the primitive prison, till man, with Promethean felicity and boldness, luckily sinned himself out of it. Thence followed Babylon, Nineveh, Venice. London, haberdashers, goldsmiths, taverns, playhouses, satires, epigrams, puns,—these all came in on the town part, and the thither side of innocence. Man found out inventions. From my den I return you condolence for your decaying sight; not for anything there is to see in the country, but for the miss of the pleasure of reading a London newspaper. The poets are as well to listen to: anything high may, nay must, be read out; you read it to yourself with an imaginary auditor; but the light paragraphs must be glid over by the proper eye; mouthing mumbles their gossamery substance. 'Tis these trifles I should mourn in fading sight. A newspaper is the single gleam of comfort I receive here; it comes from rich Cathay with tidings of mankind. Yet I could not attend to it, read out by the most beloved voice. But your eyes do not get worse, I gather. O for the collyrium of Tobias inclosed in a whiting's liver, to send you with no apocryphal good wishes! The last long time I heard from you, you had knocked your head against something. Do not do so; for your head (I do not flatter) is not a knob, or the top of a brass nail, or the end of a nine pin,—unless a Vulcanian hammer could fairly batter a "Recluse" out of it; then would

Charles Lamb

I bid the smirched god knock and knock lustily, the two-handed skinker. Mary must squeeze out a line *propriâ manu*, but indeed her fingers have been incorrigibly nervous to letter writing for a long interval. 'Twill please you all to hear, that though I fret like a lion in a net, her present health and spirits are better than they have been for some time past. She is absolutely three years and a half younger, as I tell her, since we have adopted this boarding plan.

Our providers are an honest pair, Dame W[estwood] and her husband. He, when the light of prosperity shined on them, a moderately thriving haberdasher, within Bow bells, retired since with something under a competence; writes himself parcel gentleman; hath borne parish offices; sings fine old sea songs at threescore and ten; sighs only now and then when he thinks that he has a son on his hands, about fifteen, whom he finds a difficulty in getting out into the world, and then checks a sigh with muttering, as I once heard him prettily, not meaning to be heard, "I have married my daughter, however;" takes the weather as it comes: outsides it to town in severest season; and o'winter nights tells old stories not tending to literature (how comfortable to author-rid folks!), and has *une anecdote*, upon which and about forty pounds a year he seems to have retired in green old age. It was how he was a rider in his youth, travelling for shops, and once (not to balk his employer's bargain) on a

sweltering day in August, rode foaming into
Dunstable upon a mad horse, to the dismay
and expostulatory wonderment of innkeepers,
ostlers, etc., who declared they would not have
bestrid the beast to win the Derby. Understand, the creature galled to death and despera-
tion by gad-flies, cormorant-winged, worse
than beset Inachus's daughter. This he tells,
this he brindles and burnishes on a Winter's
eve; 'tis his star of set glory, his rejuvenes-
cence, to descant upon. Far from me be it (*dii
avertant*) to look a gift story in the mouth, or
cruelly to surmise (as those who doubt the
plunge of Curtius) that the inseparate conjunc-
ture of man and beast, the centaur-phenomenon
that staggered all Dunstable, might have been
the effect of unromantic necessity; that the
horse-part carried the reasoning, willy nilly;
that needs must when such a devil drove; that
certain spiral configurations in the frame of
T[homas] W[estwood] unfriendly to alighting,
made the alliance more forcible than voluntary.
Let him enjoy his fame for me, nor let me hint
a whisper that shall dismount Bellerophon.
But in case he was an involuntary martyr, yet
if in the fiery conflict he buckled the soul of a
constant haberdasher to him, and adopted his
flames, let accident and him share the glory.
You would all like Thomas Westwood. How
weak is painting to describe a man! Say that
he stands four feet and a nail high by his own
yard measure, which, like the sceptre of Aga-

memnon, shall never sprout again, still you
have no adequate idea; nor when I tell you
that his dear hump, which I have favoured in
the picture, seems to me of the buffalo—indica-
tive and repository of mild qualities, a budget
of kindnesses—still you have not the man.
Knew you old Norris of the Temple? sixty
years ours and our father's friend? He was
not more natural to us than this old W., the
acquaintance of scarce more weeks. Under
his roof now ought I to take my rest, but that
back-looking ambition tells me I might yet be
a Londoner! Well, if we ever do move, we
have incumbrances the less to impede us; all
our furniture has faded under the auctioneer's
hammer, going for nothing, like the tarnished
frippery of the prodigal, and we have only a
spoon or two left to bless us. Clothed we came
into Enfield, and naked we must go out of it.
I would live in London shirtless, bookless.
Henry Crabb is at Rome; advices to that effect
have reached Bury. But by solemn legacy he
bequeathed at parting (whether he should live
or die) a turkey of Suffolk to be sent every
succeeding Christmas to us and divers other
friends. What a genuine old bachelor's action. I fear he will find the air of Italy too
classic. His station is in the Harz forest; his
soul is be-Goethed. Miss Kelly we never see;
Talfourd not this half-year: the latter flour-
ishes, but the exact number of his children
(God forgive me!) I have utterly forgotten.

We single people are often out in our count
there. Shall I say two? We see scarce anybody. Can I cram loves enough to you all in
this little O? Excuse particularising.

C. L.

TO WILLIAM WORDSWORTH

[End of May nearly] 1833.

Dear Wordsworth—Your letter, save in what
respects your dear sister's health, cheered me
in my new solitude. Mary is ill again. Her
illnesses encroach yearly. The last was three
months, followed by two of depression most
dreadful. I look back upon her earlier attacks
with longing: nice little durations of six weeks
or so, followed by complete restoration,—
shocking as they were to me then. In short,
half her life she is dead to me, and the other
half is made anxious with fears and lookings
forward to the next shock. With such prospects, it seemed to me necessary that she
should no longer live with me, and be fluttered
with continued removals; so I am come to
live with her, at a Mr. Walden's and his wife,
who take in patients, and have arranged to
lodge and board us only. They have had the
care of her before. I see little of her: alas!
I too often hear her. *Sunt lachrymæ rerum!*
and you and I must bear it.

To lay a little more load on it, a circumstance

has happened, *cujus pars magna fui,* and which, at another crisis, I should have more rejoiced in. I am about to lose my old and only walk-companion, whose mirthful spirits were the "youth of our house," Emma Isola. I have her here now for a little while, but she is too nervous, properly to be under such a roof, so she will make short visits,—be no more an inmate. With my perfect approval, and more than concurrence, she is to be wedded to Moxon, at the end of August—so "perish the roses and the flowers"—how is it?

Now to the brighter side. I am emancipated from the Westwoods, and I am with attentive people, and younger. I am three or four miles nearer the great city; coaches half-price less, and going always, of which I will avail myself. I have few friends left there, one or two though, most beloved. But London streets and faces cheer me inexpressibly, though not one known of the latter were remaining.

Thank you for your cordial reception of "Elia." *Inter nos,* the *Ariadne* is not a darling with me; several incongruous things are in it, but in the composition it served me as illustrative.

I want you in the "Popular Fallacies" to like the "Home that is no home," and "Rising with the lark."

I am feeble, but cheerful in this my genial hot weather. Walked sixteen miles yesterday. I can't read much in the summer time.

With my kindest love to all, and prayers for dear Dorothy,

I remain most affectionately yours,

C. LAMB.

At Mr. Walden's, Church Street, Edmonton, Middlesex.

Moxon has introduced Emma to Rogers, and he smiles upon the project. I have given E. my MILTON (will you pardon me) in part of *a portion*. It hangs famously in his Murray-like shop.

Verses

VERSES

A FAREWELL TO TOBACCO

MAY the Babylonish curse
Straight confound my stammering verse,
If I can a passage see
In this word-perplexity,
Or a fit expression find,
Or a language to my mind,
(Still the phrase is wide or scant)
To take leave of thee, GREAT PLANT!
Or in any terms relate
Half my love, or half my hate;
For I hate yet love thee so,
That, whichever thing I show,
The plain truth will seem to be
A constrain'd hyperbole,
And the passion to proceed
More from a mistress than a weed.

Sooty retainer to the vine,
Bacchus' black servant, negro fine;
Sorcerer, that mak'st us dote upon
Thy begrimed complexion,

Charles Lamb

And, for thy pernicious sake,
More and greater oaths to break
Than reclaimed lovers take
'Gainst women : thou thy siege dost lay
Much too in the female way,
While thou suck'st the lab'ring breath
Faster than kisses or than death.

Thou in such a cloud dost bind us,
That our worst foes cannot find us,
And ill fortune, that would thwart us,
Shoots at rovers, shooting at us ;
While each man, through thy heightening
    steam,
Does like a smoking Etna seem,
And all about us does express
(Fancy and wit in richest dress)
A Sicilian fruitfulness.

Thou through such a mist dost show us,
That our best friends do not know us,
And, for those allowèd features,
Due to reasonable creatures,
Liken'st us to fell Chimeras
Monsters that, who see us, fear us ;
Worse than Cerberus or Geryon,
Or, who first loved a cloud, Ixion.

Bacchus we know, and we allow
His tipsy rites. But what art thou,
That but by reflex canst show
What his deity can do,

Verses

As the false Egyptian spell
Aped the true Hebrew miracle?
Some few vapours thou may'st raise.
The weak brain may serve to amaze,
But to the reins and nobler heart
Canst nor life nor heat impart.

Brother of Bacchus, later born,
The old world was sure forlorn
Wanting thee, that aidest more
The god's victories than before
All his panthers, and the brawls
Of his piping Bacchanals.
These, as stale, we disallow,
Or judge of *thee* meant: only thou
His true Indian conquest art;
And, for ivy round his dart,
The reformèd god now weaves
A finer thyrsus of thy leaves.

Scent to match thy rich perfume
Chemic art did ne'er presume
Through her quaint alembic strain,
None so sov'reign to the brain.
Nature, that did in thee excel,
Framed again no second smell.
Roses, violets, but toys
For the smaller sort of boys,
Or for greener damsels meant;
Thou art the only manly scent.

Charles Lamb

Stinking'st of the stinking kind,
Filth of the mouth and fog of the mind,
Africa, that brags her foison,
Breeds no such prodigious poison,
Henbane, nightshade, both together,
Hemlock, aconite—

           Nay, rather,
Plant divine, of rarest virtue;
Blisters on the tongue would hurt you.
'Twas but in a sort I blamed thee;
None e'er prosper'd who defamed thee;
Irony all, and feign'd abuse,
Such as perplex'd lovers use,
At a need, when, in despair
To paint forth their fairest fair,
Or in part but to express
That exceeding comeliness
Which their fancies doth so strike,
They borrow language of dislike;
And, instead of Dearest Miss,
Jewel, Honey, Sweetheart, Bliss,
And those forms of old admiring,
Call her Cockatrice and Siren,
Basilisk, and all that's evil,
Witch, Hyena, Mermaid, Devil,
Ethiop, Wench, and Blackamoor,
Monkey, Ape, and twenty more;
Friendly Trait'ress, loving Foe,—
Not that she is truly so,
But no other way they know

A contentment to express,
Borders so upon excess,
That they do not rightly wot
Whether it be pain or not.

Or, as men constrain'd to part
With what's nearest to their heart,
While their sorrow's at the height,
Lose discrimination quite,
And their hasty wrath let fall,
To appease their frantic gall,
On the darling thing whatever,
Whence they feel it death to sever,
Though it be, as they, perforce,
Guiltless of the sad divorce.

For I must (nor let it grieve thee,
Friendliest of plants, that I must) leave thee,
For thy sake, TOBACCO, I
Would do anything but die,
And but seek to extend my days
Long enough to sing thy praise.
But, as she, who once hath been
A king's consort, is a queen
Ever after, nor will bate
Any tittle of her state,
Though a widow, or divorced,
So I, from thy converse forced,
The old name and style retain,
A right Katherine of Spain;
And a seat, too, 'mongst the joys
Of the blest Tobacco Boys;

Charles Lamb

Where, though I, by sour physician,
Am debarr'd the full fruition
Of thy favours, I may catch
Some collateral sweets, and snatch
Sidelong odours, that give life
Like glances from a neighbour's wife;
And still live in the by-places
And the suburbs of thy graces;
And in thy borders take delight,
An unconquer'd Canaanite.

SHE IS GOING

FOR their eldest Sister's hair
Martha does a wreath prepare
Of bridal rose, ornate and gay
To-morrow is the wedding day.
                    She is going.

Mary, youngest of the three,
Laughing idler, full of glee,
Arm in arm does fondly chain her,
Thinking (poor trifler!) to detain her;
                    But she's going

Vex not, maidens, nor regret
Thus to part with Margaret.
Charms like yours can never stay
Long within doors; and one day
                    You'll be going.

THE OLD FAMILIAR FACES

I HAVE had playmates, I have had companions,
In my days of childhood, in my joyful school-
days,
All, all are gone, the old familiar faces.

I have been laughing, I have been carousing,
Drinking late, sitting late, with my bosom
cronies,
All, all are gone, the old familiar faces.

I loved a love once, fairest among women;
Closed are her doors on me, I must not see
her—
All, all are gone, the old familiar faces.

I have a friend, a kinder friend has no man;
Like an ingrate, I left my friend abruptly;
Left him, to muse on the old familiar faces.

Ghost-like I paced round the haunts of my
childhood.
Earth seem'd a desert I was bound to traverse,
Seeking to find the old familiar faces.

Friend of my bosom, thou more than a brother,
Why wert not thou born in my father's dwell-
ing?
So might we talk of the old familiar faces—

Charles Lamb

How some they have died, and some they have
    left me,
And some are taken from me ; all are departed ;
All, all are gone, the old familiar faces.